COLL

Cycling

LOCH NESS
& THE SPEY VALLEY

C000184860

HarperCollins*Publishers*

Published by Collins
An imprint of HarperCollins*Publishers*
77–85 Fulham Palace Road
London W6 8JB

www.**fire**and**water**.com
www.bartholomewmaps.com

First published 2000
Copyright © HarperCollins*Publishers* Ltd 2000
Maps © Bartholomew Ltd 2000

Collins® is a registered trade mark of
HarperCollins*Publishers* Limited

Routes compiled by Julie Rattray and Ronald Chard.
Design by Creative Matters Design Consultancy, Glasgow.
Typeset by Bob Vickers.

Photographs reproduced by kind permission of the following:
Dennis Hardley pages 5, 8, 26, 37, 41, 55, 67, 93; Scottish Highland Photo Library
pages 18 (Steve Austin), 29, 63 (Steve Austin); Scotland in Focus (J Weir) page 11.

Printed in Italy

ISBN 0 00 448940 3
00/1/13

CONTENTS

KEY TO ROUTES

Route		Grade	Distance km (miles)	Time to allow	Page
1	Loch Morlich and Loch an Eilein	moderate	20 (12.5)	1–3 hours	14
2	Fochabers and Spey Bay	easy	18 (11)	2–3 hours	17
3	North Kessock and the Black Isle Wildlife Centre	strenuous	18 (11)	3 hours	20
4	River Fiddich – Craigellachie to Dufftown	moderate	18.5 (11.5)	2–3 hours	23
5	Boat of Garten and Abernethy Forest	easy	22 (13.5)	3 hours	25
6	Forres, Brodie and Culbin Forest	easy	23 (14.5)	3–4 hours	28
7	Aviemore, Kingussie and Newtonmore	moderate	28.5 (17.5)	3 hours	32
8	Elgin, Lossiemouth and Duffus Castle	easy	31.5 (19.5)	3–4 hours	36
9	Speyside Way, Glen Rinnes and Aberlour	moderate	31.5 (19.5)	3–4 hours	40
10	The Black Isle – Fortrose and Cromarty	moderate	38.5 (24)	3–4 hours	44
11	Carrbridge to Grantown-on-Spey	easy	40 (25)	4 hours	47
12	Inverness, Glen Convinth and a Loch Ness cruise	strenuous	41.5 (26)	3–4 hours	50
13	Tomintoul, Glenlivet and A'an Side	strenuous	43 (27)	4–6 hours	54
14	Beauly Firth circuit	easy	46.5 (29)	4 hours	58
15	Beauly and Strathglass	easy	57.5 (35.5)	4 hours	62
16	An Sluggan and Ryvoan Passes	strenuous	59.5 (37)	4–5 hours	66
17	Glen Feshie and Strathspey – Aviemore to Dalwhinnie	moderate	65 (40.5)	4–5 hours	70
18	Clava, Cawdor and Culloden	moderate	67.5 (42)	4–5 hours	75
19	Speyside Way and Buckie	moderate	72 (44.5)	6–8 hours	79
20	Elgin, Burghead Bay and Forres	easy	73 (45.5)	5–6 hours	84
21	Black Isle circuit	moderate	74 (46)	5–6 hours	89
22	Inverness, Foyers and Loch Ruthven	strenuous	78.5 (49)	6–7 hours	94
23	Tomintoul, Ballindalloch and the Speyside Way	moderate	80.5 (50)	6–7 hours	98
24	Nairn, Dulsie Bridge and Lochindorb	moderate	102 (63.5)	7–8 hours	102
25	Loch Ness circuit – a grande randonnée	strenuous	128 (79.5)	8–10 hours	107

Distances have been rounded up or down to the nearest 0.5km (mile).

undemanding rides compiled specifically with families in mind
15–25km (10–15 miles)

middle distance rides suitable for all cyclists
25–40km (15–25 miles)

half-day rides for the more experienced and adventurous cyclist
40–60km (25–40 miles)

challenging full-day rides
over 60km (over 40 miles)

grande randonnée – a grand cycling tour
100km (60 miles)

 Routes marked with this symbol are off-road or have off-road sections
(includes well-surfaced cycleways as well as rougher off-road tracks)

Culloden

LOCATION MAP

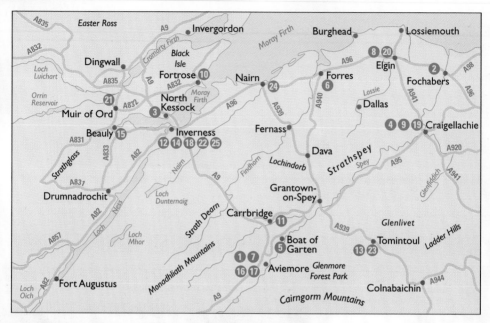

KEY TO ROUTE MAPS

M23 / Service area	Motorway		Cycle route / optional route		☎	Telephone
A259	'A' road / Dual carriageway		🚴	Start of cycle route		🜊	Picnic site
B2130	'B' road / Dual carriageway		12	Route direction		▲	Camping site
	Good minor road		B	Place of interest		👫	Public toilets
	Minor road		◼	Public house		†	Place of worship
	Track / bridleway		☕	Café / refreshments		✺	Viewpoint
	Railway / station		✗	Restaurant		⚑	Golf course
	Canal / river / loch		🍴	Convenience store		⁙	Tumulus
	Ferry route		i	Tourist Information Centre			Urban area
50	Contour (height in metres)		P	Parking			Woodland

Height above sea level

50	100	150	200	300	400	500	600	700	800	900	1000	1100	1200	1300 metres
165	330	490	655	985	1315	1645	1975	2305	2635	2965	3287	3616	3945	4274 feet

INTRODUCTION

How to use this guide

Collins' *Cycling Loch Ness & the Spey Valley* has been devised for those who want trips out on their bicycles along quiet roads and tracks, passing interesting places and convenient refreshment stops without having to devise their own routes. Each of the 25 routes in this book has been compiled and ridden by an experienced cyclist for cyclists of all abilities.

Cycling Loch Ness & the Spey Valley is easy to use. Routes range from undemanding rides compiled specifically with families in mind to challenging full-day rides; the type of route is easily identified by colour coding (see page 5). At the start of each route an information box summarises: total distance (in kilometres/miles – distances have been rounded up or down throughout to the nearest 0.5km/mile and are approximate only); grade (easy, moderate or strenuous based on distance and difficulty); terrain; an average time to allow for the route; directions to the start of the route by car and, if appropriate, by train.

Each route is fully mapped and has concise, easy-to-follow directions. Comprehensive information on places of interest and convenient refreshment stops along each route are also given. Accumulated mileages within each route description give an indication of progress, while the profile diagram is a graphic representation of gradients along the route. These should be used as a guide only.

The following abbreviations are used in the route directions:

LHF	left hand fork
RHF	right hand fork
SO	straight on
SP	signpost
TJ	T junction
TL	turn left
TR	turn right
XR	crossroads

Cycling Loch Ness & the Spey Valley

The rides in this book run through the Highlands of Scotland, covering the area from Muir of Ord in the west to Craigellachie in the east, and from Aviemore and Fort Augustus in the south to Elgin and the Black Isle in the north.

The routes stay away from busy main roads as much as possible to allow cyclists to discover the peaceful back lanes, forestry tracks, bridleways and cycleways that cross this area, passing all manner of museums, castles, historic houses and other attractions. Although the major roads are busy, particularly in summer, the back lanes have remarkably little traffic. The areas covered by these routes are still predominantly rural – many of the towns and villages have preserved their traditional character which you will see along the way. Much of this area is hilly, and there are steep sections to be tackled in some of the routes. However, this is compensated for by the spectacular views – and you can always get off and push your bike!

Various off-road routes are followed, including sections of the National Cycle Network, the Speyside Way and the Great Glen Cycle Route. Be aware that these routes are often designated as multi-use, for walkers and horse riders as well as cyclists. The National Cycle Network is being developed by the charity Sustrans and will run through towns and cities to link urban areas with the countryside. For further information write to Sustrans, 35 King Street, Bristol, BS1 4DZ, telephone (0117) 926 8893, or visit their web site at www.sustrans.org.uk. The Speyside Way is a long distance footpath running between the Cairngorm mountains and the sea, following the Spey Valley. Not all sections of the path are suitable for cyclists and the Countryside Ranger at Craigellachie can give further details, telephone (0340) 881266. The Great Glen Cycle Route follows a network of roads and tracks through forestry, minor roads and sections of the

Caledonian Canal towpath, and will eventually provide a continuous route between Fort William and Inverness. For further information contact: Forest Enterprise (01320) 366322 or (01397) 702184; British Waterways (01463) 233140; Highland Regional Council (01463) 702604; or Tourist Information Centres (see page 13).

Geology, geography and history

This beautiful area of Scotland, the Highlands, was created as a result of ancient rock movements. The entire area was covered by glaciers during the Ice Age and the movement and melting of the ice scoured out the deep valleys and lochs such as Loch Ness, Scotland's deepest loch. Much of the rock is hard granite and does not contain fossils, but the sandstone

Inverness Castle and the River Ness

around the Moray Firth and Rosemarkie in particular, formed from the sediment of ancient lakes, contains fish fossils.

The Highlands have been inhabited for over 8000 years and there is still evidence of ancient settlements and burial sites. The Scots arrived from Ireland in around 500 AD and brought with them Christianity and the Gaelic language. Throughout the following centuries the Highlands remained a separate entity from the rest of Scotland, not only because of the physical mountain barrier but also by language and custom. However, the arrival in the early 18th century of General Wade who built the first roads in the area, and the defeat of the Jacobites at the Battle of Culloden in 1746, changed the old way of life forever. The first Highland towns were built to house people cleared from the surrounding glens to make way for more profitable sheep. Other families emigrated abroad or moved to the coast to fish for herring. By the mid-19th century, the Highlands had become fashionable and the first tourists had arrived. The north–south rail links were developed and the heads of Clans and landowners were able to lease their Highland estates to sporting tenants.

Today these estates are still in operation, as well as the fishing ports and sheep farms. Commercial forestry has developed enormously, along with the tourist industry and, particularly around the Cairngorms, the winter sports facilities. And, of course, the traditional whisky industry is still going strong – this area has the greatest concentration of malt distilleries in the country.

Preparing for a cycling trip

Basic maintenance
A cycle ride is an immense pleasure, particularly on a warm sunny day. Nothing is better than coasting along a country lane gazing over the countryside. Unfortunately, not every cycling day is as perfect as this, and it is important to make sure that your bike is in good order and that you are taking the necessary clothing and supplies with you.

Before you go out on your bicycle check that everything is in order. Pump the tyres up if needed, and check that the brakes are working properly and that nothing is loose – the brakes are the only means of stopping quickly and safely. If there is a problem and you are not sure that you can fix it, take the bike to a cycle repair shop – they can often deal with small repairs very quickly.

When you go out cycling it is important to take either a puncture repair kit or a spare inner tube – it is often quicker to replace the inner tube in the event of a puncture, though it may be a good idea to practise first. You also need a pump, and with a slow puncture the pump may be enough to get you home. To remove the tyre you need a set of tyre levers. Other basic tools are an Allen key and a spanner. Some wheels on modern bikes can be removed by quick release levers built into the bike. Take a lock for your bike and if you have to leave it at any time, leave it in public view and locked through the frame and front wheel to something secure.

What to wear and take with you
It is not necessary to buy specialised cycling clothes. If it is not warm enough to wear shorts wear trousers which are easy to move in but fairly close to the leg below the knee – leggings are ideal – as this stops the trousers catching the chain. If you haven't got narrow-legged trousers, bicycle clips will hold them in. Jeans are not a good idea as they are rather tight and difficult to cycle in, and if they get wet they take a long time to dry. If your shorts or trousers are thin you might get a bit sore from being too long on the

saddle. This problem can be reduced by using a gel saddle, and by wearing thicker, or extra, pants. Once you are a committed cyclist you can buy cycling shorts; or undershorts which have a protective pad built in and which can be worn under anything. It is a good idea to wear several thin layers of clothes so that you can add or remove layers as necessary. A zip-fronted top gives easy temperature control. Make sure you have something warm and something waterproof.

If you wear shoes with a firm, flat sole you will be able to exert pressure on the pedals easily, and will have less work to do to make the bicycle move. Gloves not only keep your hands warm but protect them in the event that you come off, and cycling mittens which cushion your hands are not expensive. A helmet is not a legal requirement, but it will protect your head if you fall.

In general it is a good idea to wear bright clothing so that you can be easily seen by motorists, and this is particularly important when it is overcast or getting dark. If you might be out in the dark or twilight fit your bicycle with lights – by law your bicycle must have a reflector. You can also buy reflective bands for your ankles, or to wear over your shoulder and back, and these help motorists to see you.

You may be surprised how quickly you use up energy when cycling, and it is important to eat a carbohydrate meal before you set out. When planning a long ride, eat well the night before. You should eat small amounts of food regularly while you are cycling, or you may find that your energy suddenly disappears, particularly if there are hills or if the weather is cold. It is important to always carry something to eat with you – chocolate, bananas, biscuits – so that if you do start fading away you can restore yourself quickly. In warm weather you will sweat and use up fluid, and you always need to carry something

to drink – water will do! Many bicycles have a fitment in which to put a water bottle, and if you don't have one a cycle shop should be able to fit one.

It is also a good idea to carry a small first aid kit. This should include elastoplasts or bandages, sunburn cream, and an anti-histamine in case you are stung by a passing insect.

It is a good idea to have a pannier to carry all these items. Some fit on the handlebars, some to the back of the seat and some onto a back rack. For a day's ride you probably won't need a lot of carrying capacity, but it is better to carry items in a pannier rather than in a rucksack on your back. Pack items that you are carrying carefully – loose items can be dangerous.

Getting to the start of the ride

If you are lucky you will be able to cycle to the start of the ride, but often transport is necessary. If you travel there by train, some sprinter services carry two bicycles without prior booking. Other services carry bicycles free in off-peak periods, but check the details with your local station. Alternatively, you could use your car – it may be possible to get a bike in the back of a hatchback if you take out the front wheel. There are inexpensive, easily fitted car racks which carry bicycles safely. Your local cycle store will be able to supply one to suit you.

Cycling on-road

Cycling on back roads is a delight with quiet lanes, interesting villages, good views and a smooth easy surface to coast along on. The cycle rides in this book are mainly on quiet roads but you sometimes cross busy roads or have stretches on B roads, and whatever sort of road you are on it is essential to ride safely. Always be aware of the possibility or existence of other traffic. Glance behind regularly, signal before

Loch an Eilein, Rothiemurchus

you turn or change lane, and keep to the left. If there are motorists around, make sure that they have seen you before you cross their path. Cycling can be dangerous if you are competing for space with motor vehicles, many of which seem to have difficulty in seeing cyclists. When drivers are coming out of side roads, catch their eye before you ride in front of them.

You will find that many roads have potholes and uneven edges. They are much more difficult to spot when you are in a group because of the restricted view ahead, and therefore warnings need to be given. It is a good idea to cycle about a metre out into the road, conditions permitting, so that you avoid the worst of the uneven surfaces and to give you room to move in to the left if you are closely overtaken by a motor vehicle.

Other things to be careful of are slippery roads, particularly where there is mud or fallen leaves.

Sudden rain after a period of dry weather often makes the roads extremely slippery. Dogs, too, are a hazard because they often move unpredictably, and sometimes like to chase cyclists. If you are not happy, stop or go slowly until the problem has passed.

Pedalling

Many modern bikes have 18 or 21 gears with three rings at the front and six or seven on the back wheel, and for much of the time you will find that the middle gear at the front with the range of gears at the back will be fine. Use your gears to find one that is easy to pedal along in so that your feet move round easily and you do not put too much pressure on your knees. If you are new to the bike and the gears it is a good idea to practise changing the gears on a stretch of flat, quiet road so that when you need to change gears quickly you will be ready to do so.

Cycling in a group

When cycling in a group it is essential to do so in a disciplined manner for your own, and others', safety. Do not ride too close to the bicycle in front of you – keep about a bicycle's length between you so that you will have space to brake or stop. Always keep both hands on the handlebars, except when signalling, etc. It is alright to cycle two abreast on quiet roads, but if it is necessary to change from cycling two abreast to single file this is usually done by the outside rider falling in behind the nearside rider; always cycle in single file where there are double white lines, on busy roads, or on narrow and winding roads where you have a restricted view of the road ahead. Overtake on the right (outside) only; do not overtake on the inside.

It is important to pass information to other members of the group, for example:

car up – a vehicle is coming up behind the group and will be overtaking;

car down – a vehicle is coming towards the group;

single up – get into single file;

stopping – stopping, or

slowing/easy – slowing due to junction, etc., ahead;

on the left – there is an obstacle on the left, e.g. pedestrian, parked car;

pothole – pothole (and point towards it).

Accidents

In case of an accident, stay calm and, if needed, ring the emergency services on 999. It is a good idea to carry a basic first aid kit and perhaps also one of the commercial foil wraps to put around anyone who has an accident to keep them warm. If someone comes off their bicycle move them and the bike off the road if it is safe to do so. Get someone in the party to warn approaching traffic to slow down, and if necessary ring for an ambulance.

Cycling off-road

All the routes in this book take you along legal rights of way – bridleways, byways open to all traffic and roads used as public paths – it is illegal to cycle along footpaths. Generally the off-road sections of the routes will be easy if the weather and ground are dry. If the weather has been wet and the ground is muddy, it is not a good idea to cycle along bridleways unless you do not mind getting dirty and unless you have a mountain bike which will not get blocked up with mud. In dry weather any bicycle will be able to cover the bridleway sections, but you may need to dismount if the path is very uneven.

Off-road cycling is different to cycling on the road. The average speed is lower, you will use more energy, your riding style will be different and there is a different set of rules to obey – the off-road code:

1 Give way to horse riders and pedestrians, and use a bell or call out to warn someone of your presence.

2 Take your rubbish with you.

3 Do not light fires.

4 Close gates behind you.

5 Do not interfere with wildlife, plants or trees.

6 Use only tracks where you have a right of way, or where the landowner has given you permission to ride.

7 Avoid back wheel skids, which can start erosion gulleys and ruin the bridleway.

Some of the off-road rides take you some miles from shelter and civilisation – take waterproofs, plenty of food and drink and basic tools – especially spare inner tubes and tyre repair equipment. Tell someone where you are going and approximately when you are due back. You are more likely to tumble off your bike riding off-road, so you should consider wearing a helmet and mittens with padded palms.

Local Tourist Information Centres

Aviemore
Grampian Road, Aviemore
Telephone (01479) 810363

Carrbridge
Main Street, Carrbridge
Telephone (01479) 841630

Dufftown
The Square, Dufftown
Telephone (01340) 820501

Elgin
17 High Street, Elgin
Telephone (01343) 542666

Forres
116 High Street, Forres
Telephone (01343) 672938

Fort August
Car Park, Fort Augustus
Telephone (01320) 366367

Grantown-on-Spey
54 High Street, Grantown-on-Spey
Telephone (01479) 872773

Inverness
Castle Wynd, Inverness
Telephone (01463) 234353

Kingussie
King Street, Kingussie
Telephone (01540) 661297

Nairn
62 King Street, Nairn
Telephone (01667) 452753

North Kessock
North end of Kessock Bridge
Telephone (01463) 731505

Railia
A9 North, by Newtonmore
Telephone (01540) 673253

Tomintoul
The Square, Tomintoul
Telephone (01807) 580285

Local cycle hire

Caledonian Hotel
Inverness
Telephone (01463) 235181

Craigower Lodge Outdoor Centre
Golf Course Road, Newtonmore
Telephone (01540) 673319

Loch Insh Watersports Centre
Kincraig
Telephone (01540) 651272

M & B Stores
Boat of Garten
Telephone (01479) 831225

Also Inverdruie Mountain Bikes and Speyside Sports, see below.

Local cycle shops

Bikes of Inverness
39/41 Grant Street, Inverness
Telephone (01463) 225965

Highland Cycles
Telford Street, Inverness
Telephone (01463) 234789

Inverdruie Mountain Bikes
Rothiemurchus Visitor Centre, Inverdruie
Telephone (01479) 810787

Speyside Sports
Main Road, Aviemore
Telephone (01479) 872946

LOCH MORLICH AND LOCH AN EILEIN

Route information

Distance 20km (12.5 miles)

Grade Moderate

Terrain The main route uses the Cairngorm ski approach road, which can be busy during holiday periods, and tracks suitable for more experienced cyclists on sturdy touring or mountain bikes. However, this route can be reduced to 5km (3 miles) or, a short circuit of 6km (3.5 miles) can be followed around Loch Morlich – both of these options use only quiet, well-surfaced roads and forestry tracks, suitable for any type of bicycle. Following prolonged rain, sections of all the routes may be boggy.

Time to allow 3 hours for the main route, 2–3 hours for the shorter option; 1–2 hours for the Loch Morlich circuit.

Getting there by car Aviemore is off the A9 Perth/Inverness road. It is well signposted in both directions. There is a car park beside the railway station and the Tourist Information Centre, both of which are on the main thoroughfare. For Glenmore Forest Park Visitor Centre, go to Aviemore and then follow SP Coylumbridge/Loch Morlich/Cairngorm. The centre is 9km (5.5 miles) from Aviemore on the LHS of the road and is well signposted.

Getting there by train Aviemore is on the Glasgow/Edinburgh/Perth/Inverness line run by Scotrail. There is a frequent service and bicycles are carried free of charge – booking is essential. Telephone (0345) 484950 for enquiries.

The main route and the two shorter options follow off-road tracks through Rothiemurchus Estate and Glenmore Forest Park. The main route is an adventurous ride visiting both Loch Morlich and Loch an Eilein; the shorter option climbs gently, following tracks to the banks of Loch an Eilein before descending through Inverdruie to Aviemore. The circuit of Loch Morlich is short and flat.

Route description

Start from Aviemore railway station car park and TL onto main road.

1 Veer left into layby opposite Tourist Information Centre and join track at far end of the layby, SP Coylumbridge/Rothiemurchus. Continue on track under railway bridge. TR onto minor road running parallel to river.

2 TL and follow track across old bridge, SP Coylumbridge/Rothiemurchus. Continue to end of track (Rothiemurchus Fishery on LHS), TL and continue along main road.

3 TR to visit Rothiemurchus Visitor Centre, or SO to continue route.

4 Pass Coylumbridge Hotel and the Fun House on LHS (3km/2 miles). As road turns sharply left, TR (effectively SO) and continue on minor road (Cairngorm ski approach road). Or, if you wish to shorten the route (avoiding the Cairngorm ski approach road):

a TR with care, SP Rothiemurchus Caravan Park. Immediately TR up track (do not go into caravan park). Pass through one gate.

b SO, SP Glen Einich. Over style at next gate.

c SO at junction. Continue through one gate and then one deer fence/stile.

d SO at junction and continue to direction 11 where TR at XR.

5 TR over metal/wood bridge, through gate and follow track. (This turn is just before Loch Morlich and a parking place on RHS of road).

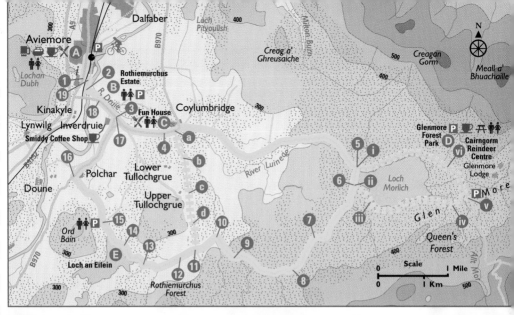

6 SO major forestry track (minor track goes off to left – the circuit of Loch Morlich could be joined here at direction ii).

7 TR onto small track, SP Piccadily/Lairig Ghru.
9.5km (6 miles)

8 SO, SP Aviemore. Follow track by river.

9 Cross Iron Bridge and TR down track.

10 TL, SP Loch an Eilein.

11 SO at XR, SP Cyclists/Loch an Eilein.

12 TR at Y junction. Continue over two small bridges beside fords.

13 TR, SP Aviemore. Continue through gate and pass red houses.
15.5 km (9.5 miles)

14 Keep right at minor junction.

15 Through barrier and rejoin tarmac beside car park. TL into car park for Loch an Eilein visitor centre, otherwise continue SO and descend.

16 TR at TJ beside Martineau Monument onto B970, SP Visitors Centre.

17 TL at TJ, onto main road, SP Aviemore.

18 At the Fishery, carefully cross road and join track, SP Aviemore. Continue on track. Cross bridge and TR onto minor road running parallel to river.

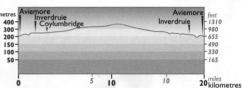

19 TL under railway bridge and climb to opposite Tourist Information Centre. TR onto main road through Aviemore, then TR into station car park to finish the route.
20 km (12.5 miles)

Loch Morlich circuit

Start from Glenmore Forest Park Visitor Centre car park (the Cairngorm Reindeer Centre is 100m along track that passes in front of the visitor centre). Descend from car park and TR onto main road – if road is busy, use track that runs alongside road. Continue.

i TL over metal/wood bridge at the end of Loch Morlich and pass through gate.

ii TL onto small track and continue on track around loch and over bridge.

iii Through gate and TL onto large forest track. SO on forest track when footpath joins from left (blue posts).

iv TL at junction (blue post) and follow track to car park by snow gates.
5km (3 miles)

v TL onto main road beside snow gates.

vi TR, SP Glenmore Forest Park Visitor Centre and complete the circuit.
6km (3.5 miles)

Places of interest along the route

A Aviemore

Aviemore, once a small Speyside village, is now a major holiday resort catering for skiers and mountaineers in the winter, walkers and cyclists in the summer. Visitors can enjoy a variety of activities, including a kart raceway, dry ski slope, off-road driving, quad driving, ice rink, swimming pools, cinema, steam railway, and the famous Santa Claus Land children's theme park. Most activities are available all year and they are all within walking distance of the start of the ride. Further information can be obtained from Aviemore Tourist Information Centre on (01479) 810363.

B Rothiemurchus Estate

Rothiemurchus is a working estate, combing farming, forestry and recreation. The estate **fishery** has a fish feeding area, tackle shop and children's play area, and instruction is available on all aspects of loch and river fishing. Ospreys may be seen between April and August. Open all year, daily 0900–1730. Admission to the fishery is free, with charge for instruction and fishing. Telephone (01479) 812345. The **visitor centre** at Inverdruie provides information on all the activities available on the estate and produces a useful visitor guide and a map for cyclists. Rangers are on hand to answer questions and give advice. Also craft and farm produce shop. Open all year, daily 0900–1730. Admission free. Telephone (01479) 810858.

C Fun House, Coylumbridge

Part of the Coylumbridge Hotel complex, the Fun House offers a range of children's activities including a soft play treehouse, 10-pin bowling, mini-golf, games area and an American diner. There is also a swimming pool on site. Open daily all year: soft play area/diner 1000–2000; golf and other games 0900–2200. Charge. Telephone (01479) 813081.

D Glenmore Forest Park, Glenmore

Glenmore Forest Park is situated in the foothills

Food and drink

There are numerous restaurants, cafés and pubs in Aviemore, and several convenience stores. Refreshments are also available at Glenmore Forest Park visitor centre.

Smiddy Coffee Shop, Inverdruie

A woodburning stove and comfy seats. Teas, coffees, homebakes, snacks and lunches available. Cyclists welcome.

Coylumbridge Hotel, Coylumbridge

As well as an American diner, the hotel has a restaurant and carvery.

of the Cairngorm National Nature Reserve, with Loch Morlich as its focal point. The area is a great haven for wildlife, including red and roe deer, pine marten, capercaillie and osprey. The Forestry Commission's **visitor centre** offers information on the many activities available, including cycling, walking, skiing, sailing and fishing. Also audio-visual presentation and displays on local history. Café with views over the loch and the mountains. Picnic area. Open all year, daily. Admission free. Telephone (01479) 861220). At the **Cairngorm Reindeer Centre** visitors can take guided walks to see the country's only free-ranging herd of reindeer. Also audio-visual presentation and exhibition. Visitor centre open Easter to October, daily 1000–1700, otherwise 1100–1700; tours to the reindeer available Easter to October, 1100 and 1430. Telephone (01479) 861228.

E Loch an Eilein

Part of Rothiemurchus Estate, Loch an Eilein was on an ancient Highland road. In the centre of the loch is a 13th-century castle. A visitor centre provides information on the surrounding countryside and there are spectacular views of the loch and surrounding mountains. The seasonal gift shop sells sweets and ice cream. Open all year, daily 0930–1730. Admission free. Telephone (01479) 812345.

Route information

Distance   18km (11 miles)

Grade   Easy

Terrain   Well-surfaced roads and a section of track along the Speyside Way, suitable for any type of bicycle. The roads are flat and quiet, making for ideal family cycling.

Time to allow   2–3 hours.

Getting there by car   Fochabers is on the A96 Aberdeen to Inverness road. The route starts from the western side of the town beside the park, SP Crazy Golf/Putting. There is car parking just off the main road beside the park.

Getting there by train   There is no practical railway access to this ride. The nearest railway stations are in Keith (12.5km/8 miles) and Elgin (14.5km/9 miles).

Following the east bank of the River Spey from Fochabers to Tugnet and Spey Bay, the route passes Dallachy, the site of a World War II air base from where the North Sea shipping lanes and the Norwegian fjords were patrolled. It then follows a small section of the Speyside Way, along traditional fisherman's footpaths, crossing the Spey Viaduct to Garmouth (for more information on the Speyside Way, see page 8). The route returns to Fochabers along the west bank of the Spey, through the village of Mosstodloch – home of Baxters Foods. Allow extra time for visiting the places of interest.

Places of interest along the route

A Fochabers Folk Museum, Fochabers

The museum, located in an old church at the east end of the High Street, illustrates the history of Fochabers over the past 200 years and includes a large collection of horse drawn carts. Gift shop. Open all year, summer 0930–1300 and 1400–1800; winter closes 1700. Admission free. Telephone (01343) 821204.

B Spey Bay

Tugnet, at Spey Bay, has been a fishing station for centuries and the old ice house contains a permanent exhibition illustrating salmon fishing and local life. **Tugnet Ice House** is a relic of the time when salmon were packed for delivery by rail throughout Britain. It sits at the mouth of the River Spey where salmon are still fished by both the local residents and ospreys. Open May (first Saturday) to September (last Saturday), daily 1100–1600. Admission free. Telephone (01309) 673701. Adjacent to the ice house is **Moray Firth Wildlife Centre**. The centre has exhibitions on the Moray Firth dolphins and hosts various children's activities, wildlife talks and dolphin watches. It is an excellent location for studying the birdlife of the Spey estuary. Picnic area and wildlife garden. Open March to October, daily 1030–1930; November and December, weekends only 1030–1700. Charge. Telephone (01343) 820339.

C Garmouth

Garmouth is traditionally known as the place where King Charles II (1630–85) landed from Belgium in 1650 to take on the armies of Oliver Cromwell. Just outside Garmouth, at Kingston, is **Lein Nature Reserve** and picnic site (access at all reasonable times). **Barnyard Studios** specialise in textiles, jewellery, stained glass and paint design. Small tearoom and pondside picnic area. Open all year, Saturday–Wednesday 1300–1600; during the summer, daily 1300–1600 (closed Fridays). Telephone (01343) 870599/870202 to confirm times, as they do vary.

Ⓓ Baxters Visitor Centre, Mosstodloch

Baxters Visitor Centre tells the history of Baxters Foods over the past 130 years. Through factory tours, audio-visual presentations, the Old Shop Museum and a range of gift shops, visitors gain an insight into the business. Also demonstration events throughout the year. The restaurant offers stunning panoramic views of the Spey and a full range of snacks and meals, with seating inside and out. Open daily (except Christmas and New Year), 0900–1730. Factory tours at weekends only. Admission free. Telephone (01343) 820666.

Spey Bay

Start from the car park at the western end of Fochabers (on the A96, SP Crazy Golf/Putting). Cycle through car park and follow the track that runs down the side of the Water Authority building/enclosure. Take RHF and continue under old and new bridge. TR and cross mound using steps/ramp and continue on path (0.5km/0.3 mile).

1   At Speyside Way information board, TL to join road (B9104) and continue.

2   SO (Speyside Way SP pointing left), continuing on B9104 (1.5km/1 mile).

3   Pass memorial to Dallachy Strike Wing on RHS.   *5km (3 miles)*

4   Pass Spey Bay Post Office on RHS.

5   SO, SP Spey Bay.

6   Veer left at Spey Bay Hotel and follow SP for car park.

7   Enter car park. Tugnet Ice House is SO. Moray Firth Wildlife Centre is on RHS. Leave car park and follow SP Speyside Way/Toilets to join track. Pass between river and ice house and a row of houses.

8   TR down a good farm track, SP Speyside Way.   *8km (5 miles)*

9   SO, SP Speyside Way (TL is farm track).

10   TR at old bridge remains, down good track, SP Spey Bay Wildlife Reserve/Scottish Wildlife Trust.

11   Veer left up track onto old railway viaduct and cross River Spey. Rejoin track and continue under two bridges with gates.
10km (6 miles)

12   Track joins car park after second bridge. TL up small track to visit Barnyard Studios, or to continue route, pass through car park and TR onto road.

13 TL, SP Garmouth ½ B9015 and continue on South Road into Garmouth.

14 Pass Garmouth Inn. If you veer left here, you can cycle through Garmouth to the public park and play area (on LHS) to see the house where King Charles II stayed on his arrival from Belgium (plaque on wall on house on RHS of road). Continue 1km (0.6 mile) further down this dead end road to Kingston, for Lein Nature Reserve.

Otherwise, to continue route, TR, SP Fochabers 4, Lemanfield ¼, and continue along Church Road to Mosstodloch.

15 Enter Mosstodloch (play area on RHS).
15.5km (9.5 miles)

16 TL at TJ, no SP, to join the busy A96 Inverness to Aberdeen road – children should cycle on the shared use path that runs adjacent to the road. Pass Ben Aigan Hotel on the LHS.

17 To visit Baxters Visitor Centre, TL, SP Baxters Visitor Centre, and immediately TR into car park. On leaving visitor centre, retrace to A96 and TR to rejoin the shared use cycle path, staying on the same side of the road as Baxters until the pelican crossing and continue as below.

Otherwise, continue to pelican crossing and cross A96. TL to follow cycle path into Fochabers.

18 SO over tarmac road and rejoin cycle path. Cross old Spey Bridge and continue on path.

19 Continue through gate at end of track and TR into car park, SP Crazy Golf/Putting, to complete the route. *18km (11 miles)*

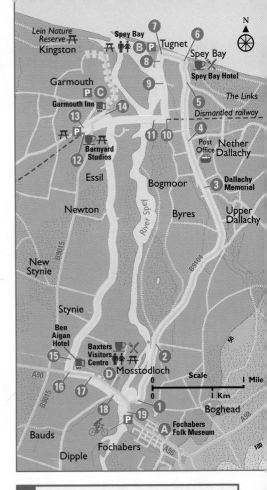

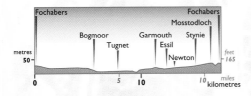

Food and drink

Refreshments are available at Barnyard Studios and Baxters Visitor Centre.

Spey Bay Hotel, Spey Bay
Hotel offering morning coffees, afternoon teas, lunches, snacks and main meals. Open all day.

Garmouth Inn, Garmouth
Village inn with a large beer garden. Excellent pub meals and snacks. Beautiful garden in the summer. Children welcome.

NORTH KESSOCK AND THE BLACK ISLE WILDLIFE CENTRE

Route information

 Distance   18km (11 miles)

Grade   Strenuous

Terrain   Well-surfaced roads and forestry tracks, suitable for any type of bicycle with low gears and good brakes. The roads are quiet, making for ideal family cycling. There are, however, some long climbs. The main route is suitable for older children who can cope with the hills and longer distances. The route can be shortened to 8km (5 miles), but will still be hilly.

Time to allow   3 hours.

Getting there by car   North Kessock is just off the A9 on the northern side of the Kessock Bridge, 4.5km (3 miles) from Inverness. It is well signposted in both directions. There is parking on the sea front, opposite the Kessock Hotel.

Getting there by train   The nearest station is in Inverness. A designated cycle route runs from Inverness to North Kessock, along the eastern bank of the River Ness. TR out of station onto main road and continue to roundabout. Take third exit (Shore Street) and follow this road (becomes Cromwell Road then Longman Drive) as it follows shore to Kessock Bridge. Continue on cycle lane across Kessock Bridge and into North Kessock.

From North Kessock, via a designated cycle route, to Ord Hill. An optional cycle around Ord Hill is undulating, but the climbing is rewarded by magnificent views over the Beauly and Moray Firths and Inverness. A climb to Black Isle Wildlife Centre is followed by a long descent to Munlochy (although the route can be shortened by returning to North Kessock from this point). The return from Munlochy is fairly flat and follows a designated cycle route to North Kessock, using sections of the old A9. Allow extra time to visit the wildlife centre.

Route description

Start from the car park in North Kessock (opposite the Kessock Hotel). TL out of car park onto the main road (which leads you away from the Kessock Bridge). Continue to climb through North Kessock until you are almost at the A9.

1   TL 50m before the A9, Tore cycle SP. Then TR, cycle through underpass, and TR, Munlochy cycle SP.

2   TL, Munlochy cycle SP, to join the road. Climb.

3   TR, SP Kilmuir 3 miles.

4   Follow road around sharp left hand corner.

5   For optional forestry track around Ord Hill, TR, SP Ord Hill Forestry Commission Orienteering and parking. Start climbing the track:

a   TR through gate, following blue marker pole. Follow the main track around Ord Hill – excellent views over the Moray Firth, the Beauly Firth and Inverness.

b   Through gate, TR and descend.

c   TR at TJ with road, and continue to direction 6.

Or, SO to continue route.

6   TL, no SP (SO is SP dead end road).

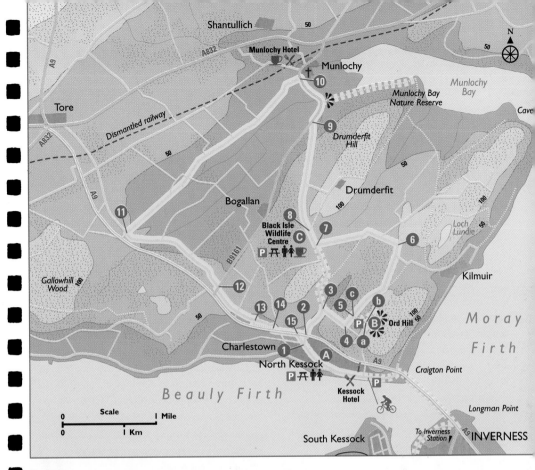

7 TR, no SP, (back SP Kilmuir 3).
5km (3 miles)

8 To visit Black Isle Wildlife Centre, TL. To shorten the route, TR out of the wildlife centre and descend – retrace route back into North Kessock. Otherwise, continue SO, then veer left down to junction.

9 TR at TJ, no SP, for a descent to Munlochy (7km/4.5 miles). As you descend, a right turn just before the bridge takes you along a track to Munlochy Bay nature reserve – home to a vast range of waterfowl.

10 TL opposite the church, just before Munlochy, no SP (Munlochy Hotel is 100m SO). Continue on this road.

11 TL at TJ, no SP (SP back the way is Munlochy cycle SP). **12.5km (8 miles)**

12 TR, North Kessock/Inverness cycle SP. Then, TL, North Kessock/Inverness cycle SP. Descend.

13 TR on track through bushes, North Kessock/Inverness cycle SP (at foot of descent just before climb). Follow track as it runs parallel to A9. **15.5km (9.5 miles)**

14 TR down to underpass, North Kessock/ Inverness cycle SP. At other end of underpass, TL along road.

15 TR at TJ and descend into North Kessock. Then, TR into car park to complete the route.

If returning to Inverness Station, TL Kessock Bridge/Inverness cycle SP and retrace route across bridge and alongside Beauly Firth back into Inverness. **18km (11 miles)**

Places of interest along the route

A North Kessock

North Kessock sits facing the narrows between the Beauly Firth and the Moray Firth. There are two wildlife exhibitions. The Moray Firth dolphins (130 individual dolphins have been identified) are one of only three known resident populations along the British coastline. **Dolphin and Seals of the Moray Firth** enables visitors to watch for these mammals, and to listen to the mysterious sounds they make via underwater microphones. Also interactive computer displays and a bulletin board with up to the minute sightings. Minke whales may be seen between August and October. Telephone (01463) 731866 for further information. Red Kites had disappeared from Scotland by 1879 but were reintroduced in 1989. The **Red Kite Viewing Centre**, at the Tourist Information Centre, allows visitors the unique opportunity of viewing live (and recorded) pictures of red kites nesting in the local area via closed circuit television. RSPB staff are available to give further information on the birds. Telephone (01463) 731505. Open daily 1000–1700; extended hours in July and August; closed Monday in winter. Admission free. To access the exhibitions, walk up the steps between the post office and the Spar shop in North Kessock (it is not feasible to take bicycles up the steps and the only other access is via the very busy A9 dual carriageway).

B Ord Hill

The track around Ord Hill (Forestry Commission property), a popular local walk and bike ride, provides excellent views over the Moray Firth, the Beauly Firth and Inverness. There is a vitrified fort on top of the hill. Also orienteering course, with numbered and lettered checkpoints. Access at all reasonable times. Admission free. Telephone (01463) 791575.

C Black Isle Wildlife Centre

The wildlife centre is home to many animals and birds including goats, rabbits, pot bellied pigs, llamas, cattle, ducks, deer, pheasants, geese and swans. Also handling and hatching areas, opportunities to feed the animals and a small train ride. There is also a 5000-year-old burial cairn on the site. Tearoom and picnic area. Open March to September, daily 1000–1800. Charge. Telephone (01463) 731656.

Food and drink

There is a tearoom at the Black Isle Wildlife Centre.

Kessock Hotel, North Kessock
Hotel serving a range of snacks and meals with veranda seating overlooking the Beauly Firth. Children welcome. The Kessock Hotel also runs boat trips to view the seals and dolphins.

Munlochy Hotel, Munlochy
Teas, coffees and lunch time bar meals. Special children's menu. Open all year.

```
metres  North Kessock              North Kessock   feet
150                                                 490
100                                                 330
50                                                  165
      0              5       10              10   miles
                                                 kilometres
```

RIVER FIDDICH – CRAIGELLACHIE TO DUFFTOWN

Route information

Distance 18.5km (11.5 miles)

Grade Moderate

Terrain Well-surfaced roads and an old railway line (part of the Speyside Way), suitable for any type of bicycle. The roads are quiet – ideal family cycling – with some gradual climbs. The return route is more strenuous, suitable for older children with good road sense. However, the Speyside Way section of the ride, between Craigellachie and Dufftown, is suitable for all family members and can be used as an alternative return route.

Time to allow 2–3 hours.

Getting there by car The route starts at Boat of Fiddich car park, Craigellachie – from Elgin, follow the A941 SP Perth and take the exit SP Keith A95; from Grantown-on-Spey, follow the A95 SP Keith/Elgin and take the exit SP Keith A95. Pass through Craigellachie and TR, SP Fiddich Park/Speyside Way Visitor Centre (100m before Fiddichside Inn and bridge).

Getting there by train There is no practical railway access to this ride. The nearest stations are Keith (19km/12 miles) and Elgin (21km/ 13 miles).

The route initially follows the Dufftown spur of the Speyside Way, before climbing into Dufftown (the whisky capital). A further gradual climb follows the eastern bank of the River Fiddich to the small village of Maggieknockater. There is a final short ascent before a long descent back to the River Fiddich and Craigellachie. The spur is part of the old Strathspey railway which ran south east, following the River Fiddich from Craigellachie to Dufftown, and linked with the whisky train between Dufftown and Keith. The track is rich in wildflowers and affords spectacular views over the River Fiddich. For more information on the Speyside Way see page 8.

Places of interest along the route

A **Speyside Way Visitor Centre, Boat of Fiddich, Craigellachie**
For information on the Speyside Way and its natural history. The Countryside Ranger can provide advice for users of the route. Opening times vary. Admission free. Telephone the ranger on (01340) 881266 for information.

B **Dufftown**
Dufftown is the centre of the whisky industry – seven distilleries were constructed here between 1823 and 1898. **Glenfiddich Distillery** produces the only Highland whisky to be chateau-bottled (bottled at the distillery). Audio-visual presentation, exhibition, gift shop and picnic area. Open January to mid-December, Monday–Friday 0930–1630; also Easter to mid-October, Saturday 0930–1630, Sunday 1200–1630. Admission free. Telephone (01340) 820373. **Balvenie Castle** was visited by King Edward I and Mary, Queen of Scots, and was occupied by the Duke of Cumberland in 1746, during the Jacobite rising. Gift shop and

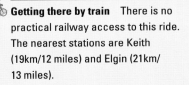

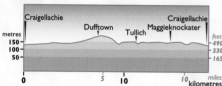

5   To visit the distillery and castle, TL SP Glenfiddich Distillery/Balvenie Castle. For the distillery, TR, SP Glenfiddich Distillery; for the castle, continue for 100m and TR. From Balvenie Castle, TL and retrace to A921.

Groups with young children may wish to retrace the route to the car park/picnic site beside Convalmore Distillery (direction 3) and follow the Speyside Way back to Craigellachie. This is easier and more suitable for inexperienced children.

To continue route, TL at TJ, SP Town Centre ¹/₂ mile (plus other local SP). Climb into Dufftown.   **8.5km (5 miles)**

6   TL at TJ, SP Rhynie A920/Keith B9014.

7   TL, SP Keith B9014, and continue.

8   TL, SP Maggieknockater, and continue alongside River Fiddich to Maggieknockater.
    10km (6 miles)

9   TL at TJ, SP Craigellachie/Grantown on Spey A95, and continue on A95.
    15km (9.5 miles)

10   Cross River Fiddich beside the Fiddichside Inn and continue for 100m. TL, SP Speyside Way, into the car park to complete the route.   **18.5km (11.5 miles)**

picnic area. Historic Scotland property. Open April to September, Monday–Saturday 0930–1830, Sunday 1400–1830. Charge. Telephone (01340) 820121.

Route description

Start from Boat of Fiddich Car Park, Craigellachie. At the Speyside Way XR SP (beside the toilets), follow the track SP Dufftown.

1   Pass playhouse and park area and continue on track.

2   Cross the River Fiddich over Newton Bridge and continue.

3   Follow track through gate, past Convalmore Distillery, to car park/picnic site. **5.5km (3.5 miles)**

4   From car park, TL onto main road (A941). Pass the old Keith and District Railway line on LHS.

Food and drink

Plenty of choice in Dufftown.

🍺 **Craigellachie Inn, Craigellachie**
Traditional hotel. Access from Speyside Way in Craigellachie (200m from Fiddich Park along Tomintoul route).

✗ **Highlander Inn, Craigellachie**
Meals are served in the bar, on the veranda overlooking the River Spey or in the dining room.

✗ **Taste of Speyside, Dufftown**
Offering the best of local produce – seafood, venison and steaks.

BOAT OF GARTEN AND ABERNETHY FOREST

Route information

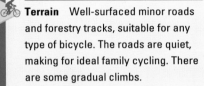

Distance   22km (13.5 miles)

Grade   Easy

Terrain   Well-surfaced minor roads and forestry tracks, suitable for any type of bicycle. The roads are quiet, making for ideal family cycling. There are some gradual climbs.

Time to allow   3 hours.

Getting there by car   Boat of Garten is 10km (6 miles) north east of Aviemore. Turn off the A95 and follow SP for Boat of Garten. The start of the route, Boat of Garten Station, is in the centre of the village beside the Boat Hotel. There is parking beside the hotel or on the other side of the railway bridge.

Getting there by train   Cyclists can use the Strathspey Steam Railway to get to Boat of Garten Station. The railway runs a passenger service from Aviemore to Boat of Garten, with around five services a day during the summer months. Bicycles are carried free if accompanied. Groups of cyclists should telephone in advance. Telephone (01479) 810725 for further information.

From Boat of Garten and across the River Spey to the Abernethy Forest. The forest is a remnant of the ancient Caledonian pine forest that once covered the Strathspey area. Interspersed with lochs, bogs and moorland, the reserve has become a haven for wildlife, including ospreys. The route loops through the forest, gradually climbing and then descending into Nethy Bridge, before returning to Boat of Garten. Allow extra time to visit Loch Garten Osprey Centre.

Places of interest along the route

Ⓐ Strathspey Steam Railway, Boat of Garten
Strathspey Steam Railway runs steam and diesel trains the 8.5km (5 miles) between Boat of Garten and Aviemore. Boat of Garten Station is beautifully restored to its Victorian splendour and a steam train journey transports passengers back to a less hurried pace of life. Special events throughout the year. Open end March to end October (and for Christmas events). Charge. Telephone (01479) 810725.

Ⓑ Loch Garten Osprey Centre and Forest Walks
The Royal Society for the Protection of Birds has a visitor centre at Loch Garten. From the centre and associated hides, utilising live pictures from a video camera close to the nests, visitors can see ospreys nesting and hunting. The lochside forest walks take visitors through the ancient Caledonian pine forest abundant in birds, flowers and insects. Organised events throughout the year. Osprey Centre open April to August, Monday–Saturday 1000–1800. Walks open all year. Gift shop. Admission free. Telephone (01479) 831476/831694.

Strathspey Steam Railway

Food and drink

Boat Hotel, Boat of Garten

Hotel and lounge bar serving lunches 1215–1415, evening meals 1800–2100. Children welcome and special children's menu.

Pollyanna's Tearoom, Nethy Bridge

Homebakes, snacks and meals. Cyclists welcome. Open end February to end October, Tuesday to Sunday (closed Monday).

Route description

Start from Boat of Garten station. TR in front of the Boat Hotel, and join main road through Boat of Garten.

1 Keep right as road veers round to right. Descend and cross River Spey. Tremendous views to west over Cairngorm mountains.

2 SO at TJ, into Garten Wood car park.

3 At back of car park, join red forest trail and follow through forest.

4 Keep left at junction – follow red trail (1.5km/1 mile).

5 TR at TJ and rejoin tarmac road (3km/2 miles).

6 Pass Loch Garten car park and forest walks on RHS.

7 To visit Loch Garten Osprey Centre, TL (5km/3 miles). Otherwise, continue SO.

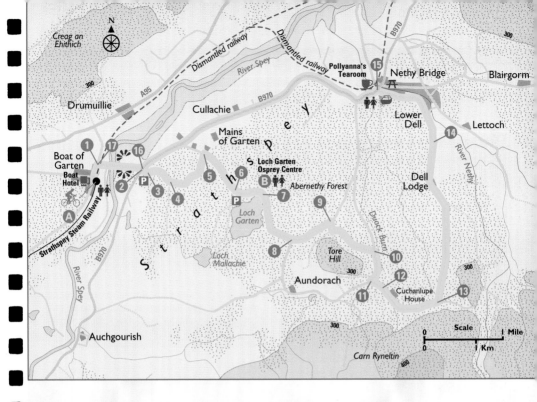

8 Keep left, SP Nethy Bridge 2¹/4.

9 TR through barrier onto forest track (at top of hill before big dip – 7km/4.5 miles). Continue for 50m and TL at track junction.

10 Through barrier, TR at TJ and join tarmac road for gradual descent.

11 Before road swings to right, TL up well-groomed sand forest trail, no SP. Continue over wooden bridge after 50m.
8.5km (5 miles)

12 Pass Cuchanlupe House and track. Pass two tracks on left.

13 TL down well-groomed track (wooden cross gate, fire beaters), SP on tree 'no heavy vehicles' (10km/6 miles). This track is half-way up a straight hill – if you get to the huts you have gone too far. Continue straight down track, passing two tracks on right, and through gate.

14 Rejoin tarmac and continue into Nethy Bridge.

15 TL onto road at TJ beside bridge and shop. Pass sports field and continue on B970 out of Nethy Bridge.
15.5km (9.5 miles)

16 TR, SP Boat of Garten ³/4 mile. Cross River Spey.
21km (13 miles)

17 LHF and continue through Boat of Garten. TL in front of the Boat Hotel into railway station to complete route.
22km (13.5 miles)

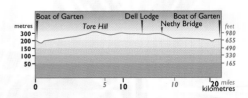

FORRES, BRODIE AND CULBIN FOREST

Route information

 Distance   23km (14.5 miles)

Grade   Easy

 Terrain   Well-surfaced roads and forestry tracks, suitable for any sturdy bicycle. The roads are quiet and generally flat, making the route suitable for all cyclists, including children who can cope with the distance.

 Time to allow   3–4 hours.

Getting there by car   Forres is on the A96 Inverness to Aberdeen road. Leave the A96 at the Forres exit. Grant Park, the start of the route, is at the eastern edge of Forres, SP Car Park/Nelson Tower. There is parking here and at the railway station.

Getting there by train   Forres is on the Aberdeen to Inverness line run by Scotrail. There is a frequent service and bicycles are carried for free – booking is essential. For enquiries telephone (0345) 484950. To join the route from the station, follow the pedestrian SP and cross the A96 Forres ring road. Follow the road to the roundabout and join the route at direction 1, where TR, SP Grantown A940.

From Grant Park in Forres, along minor roads to the River Findhorn and on through the villages of Dyke and Brodie. The route then loops through Kintessack (with an optional trip to Culbin Forest adding 6.5km/4 miles to the total distance) and follows the Inverness to Aberdeen cycle route, over the Broom of Moy bailey bridge, back to Forres. Allow extra time to visit Brodie Castle and Culbin Forest/Sands.

Places of interest along the route

A Forres

The ancient town of Forres is the main setting of Shakespeare's *Macbeth*, and the first encounter with the three witches is supposed to have taken place in the town. **Nelson Tower**, Grant Park, was built by the Trafalgar Club to commemorate Nelson's victory at Trafalgar, and first opened in 1812. There are displays on the life of the club, Lord Nelson and Forres. From the top of the tower there are spectacular views over the Moray Firth. Open May to September, Tuesday–Sunday 1400–1600. Admission free. Telephone (01309) 673701. The **Falconer Museum**, Tolbooth Street, was founded in 1871 and contains a wealth of local heritage, with displays on the early history of Moray, local archaeology, history and climate. Also the story of the Corries folk group. Open April to October, Monday–Saturday 1000–1700; November to March, Monday–Friday only. Admission free. Telephone (01309) 673701. **Sueno's Stone**, standing over 6m (20 feet) high, is located at the east end of the town. The sculptured monument, dating from the 9th or

10th century, is believed to commemorate a battle between the Picts and the Scots. Access at all reasonable times. Free of charge. Telephone Historic Scotland on 0131 668 8800 for further information. **Dallas Dhu Distillery** (not passed on this route) is also in Forres – see route 20.

B Brodie

Brodie Castle is a typical Z plan tower. Many rooms have unusual plaster ceilings, and there are fine collections of art, porcelain and furniture. The extensive grounds contain more than 400 varieties of flowers, many planted between 1890 and 1940 by the 24th Brodie of Brodie. At the entrance to the castle grounds is the Rodney Stone, a Pictish stone carved between 500 and 1000 AD. National Trust for Scotland property. Tearoom and picnic area. Open daily April to September and weekends in October, Monday–Saturday 1100–1730, Sunday 1330–1730. Charge. Telephone (01309) 641371. At

Small World, Darnaway Visitor Centre, visitors can watch artists creating miniature figurines and can have a go at painting their own. Extensive children's play area and indoor and outdoor activity areas. Tearoom. Open all year, Tuesday–Sunday and Bank Holidays 1030–1630. Telephone (01309) 641677.

C Culbin Forest and Sands

Culbin Forest (Forestry Commission property) is a designated Site of Special Scientific Interest, with the highest sand dune system in Britain, over 550 different species of flowering plants and more than 130 species of lichen. The open spaces and trees are home to roe deer, badgers, red squirrels, wildcats, pine martins and otters. There are numerous tracks through the forest and leaflets and maps are available. Access at all reasonable times. Admission free. Telephone (01343) 820223. The RSPB has a reserve on the extensive saltmarshes at Culbin. Telephone (01463) 715000 for further information.

River Findhorn

Route description

Start from East End car park, beside Grant Park, and TL onto main road. Continue along High Street, passing Falconer Museum on LHS.

1 TL at roundabout, SP Grantown A940.

2 TR, WITH CARE, SP Caravans and Camping.

3 TR, no SP (house ahead and open fields on right). ***3km (2 miles)***

4 TR, no SP.

5 Arrive TJ with A96. Cross road and TL to follow footpath over River Findhorn (5km/ 3 miles). TR for 100m, SP Kintessack/Earnhill House.

6 TL and continue parallel to railway.

7 TR, SP Dyke/Kintessack. Continue on this road, passing Dyke Church on LHS.

8 Arrive XR. To visit Brodie Castle TR (extra 0.5km/0.3 mile). After visit leave along one way system, TR and rejoin route at direction 9).

To visit Small World (extra 2km/1 mile) TL. Then TR at TJ and immediately TL. Continue to visitor centre. After visit, retrace route and continue to direction 9.

9 TR at TJ. ***10.5km (6.5 miles)***

To visit Brodie Countryfare, TL across level crossing and walk right for 100m. After visit, retrace to road and TL.

10 Pass woodland walks and picnic area on LHS.

11 TR at TJ, SP Kintessack/Culbin Sands, and cycle into forest.

12 SO to continue route.

13.5km (8.5 miles)

For Culbin Forest/Sands option, TL onto poled forestry track (first on entering forest). Go through barrier and follow main track.

a TL at TJ, SP Culbin Forest Parking. SO through car park.

b RHF at junction 34 (Y junction). Continue SO main track.

c TR at junction 18 (access to Culbin Sands at corner).

d SO at junction 15 (TL for Culbin Sands).

e TR at junction 14.

f Keep left as track goes to right.

g TR at junction 40.

h TL at TJ by junction 39.

i TR at junction 41.

j SO at junction 43, through poled gate and car park to continue on road. TL at TJ, SP Broom of Moy/Kincorth/Forres, and rejoin route at direction 14, but keep left to follow SP Broom of Moy/Kincorth/Forres.

13 TL at TJ, SP Kintessack, and cycle through Kintessack. ***16km (10 miles)***

14 Keep right and follow SP Broom of Moy/Kincorth/Forres.

15 Veer right, SP Broom of Moy/Forres and Bike SP 1.

16 TL, SP Broom of Moy and Bike SP 1.

17 Veer right at village, Bike SP 1, and cross bailey bridge. TL and follow track for 200m. At first fork take LHF for 400m. At second fork (beside river) take RHF.

18 TR at TJ beside transmitter and rejoin road, Bike SP 1.

19 TR at TJ, across level crossing. Immediately veer left up path and use pedestrian crossing to cross busy A96 Forres ring road. Rejoin road on far side of crossing.

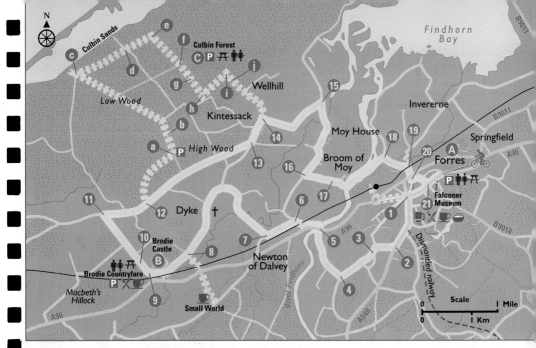

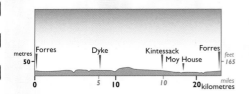

metres
50 —

Forres   Dyke   Kintessack   Forres
                                             feet
                              Moy House   165

0   5   10   10   20 kilometres
                                        miles

20 TL over small bridge and immediately TR to pass in front of Tescos. Continue up hill beside the church.

21 TL at TJ onto High Street (opposite Tourist Information Centre). Continue along High Street and TR into car park, beside Grant Park, to complete the route. *23km (14.5 miles)*

Food and drink

There are restaurants, cafés, pubs and convenience stores in Forres, and tea-rooms at Brodie Castle and Small World.

Brodie Countryfare, Brodie
Traditional restaurant featuring local Scottish ingredients on an extensive menu. Tea, coffee and snacks also available. Open all year.

AVIEMORE, KINGUSSIE AND NEWTONMORE

Route information

Distance 28.5km (17.5 miles)

Grade Moderate

Terrain Well-surfaced minor roads, with some climbing, suitable for any bicycle. The route is more suited to cyclists with some experience.

Time to allow 3 hours.

Getting there by car Aviemore is off the A9 Perth/Inverness road. It is well signposted in both directions. There is a car park beside the railway station and the Tourist Information Centre, both of which are on the main thoroughfare.

Getting there by train The start of the route, Aviemore, is on the Glasgow/Edinburgh/Perth/Inverness line run by Scotrail. There is a frequent rail service and bicycles are carried free of charge – booking is essential. Telephone (0345) 484950 for information.

This is a one way route, returning to Aviemore by train from either Kingussie (23km/14.5 miles away) or Newtonmore (travel details as above). The route follows the River Spey from Aviemore to Newtonmore, initially on the undulating eastern bank, through Inshriach Forest and across the spectacular Feshie Bridge, where the River Feshie joins the River Spey. On past Loch Insh to follow the flatter western bank of the Spey to Kingussie and Newtonmore, where the folk museums provide a fascinating insight into Highland life. Allow extra time to visit the places of interest along the route.

Places of interest along the route

Ⓐ Aviemore

Aviemore, once a small Speyside village, is now a major holiday resort catering for skiers and mountaineers in the winter, walkers and cyclists in the summer. Visitors can enjoy a variety of activities on offer, including a kart raceway, dry ski slope, off-road driving, quad driving, ice rink, swimming pools, cinema, steam railway, and the famous Santa Claus Land children's theme park. Most activities are available all year and they are all within walking distance of the start of the ride. Telephone the Tourist Information Centre in Aviemore (01479 810363) for information.

Ⓑ The Fishery, Rothiemurchus Estate

The estate fishery with fish feeding area, tackle shop and children's play area. Ospreys may be seen between April and August. Instruction is available on all aspects of loch and river fishing. Rothiemurchus Estate also has a visitor centre in Inverdruie and offers various other activities. Open all year, daily 0900–1730. Admission to the fishery is free, with charge for instruction and fishing. Telephone (01479) 812345.

Ⓒ Loch Insh Water Sports

On the shores of Loch Insh, the centre offers a

range of water sports and instruction. Also beach picnic areas, a children's adventure area and climbing wall, an interpretive trail, dry ski slope, archery and mountain bike trails. Open Easter to October, daily 0830–1730. Admission free, charge for activities and instruction. Telephone (01540) 651272.

ⓓ Highland Wildlife Park, near Kincraig

Scotland's native species (many now extinct in the wild) in their natural habitats, including red and roe deer, highland cattle, bison, Pzrewalski's horses, boar, otters, eagles and wolves. Visitors drive round the park (cyclists and walkers are driven by park staff) and then are free to wander in themed habitats. Organised events throughout the year. Coffee shop (open April to August) and picnic area. Open daily all year, weather permitting: April to October 1000–1800; June to August 1000–1900; November to March 1000–1600. Charge (reduced rates in winter). Telephone (01540) 651270.

ⓔ Highland Folk Museum

The two sites, Am Fasgadh in Kingussie and Turus Tim in Newtonmore, offer an insight into the life of the Highland crofter over the last three centuries. There are reconstructed crofts, an open air museum and live craft demonstrations. Also picnic areas, woodland and farm walks. Am Fasgadh open May to August, Monday–Saturday 1000–1730, Sunday 1300–1700; September to October, Monday–Friday 1000–1730. Turus Tim open May to August, Monday–Friday 1100–1700. Charge. Telephone (01540) 661307. For other attractions in Kingussie, see route 17.

ⓕ Waltzing Waters, Newtonmore

Elaborate water, light and music spectacular. Coffee shop and children's play area. Open all year, daily with shows on the hour between 1000 and 1600. Charge. Telephone (01540) 673752.

Food and drink

There is plenty of choice in Aviemore and Newtonmore. Refreshments are also available at the Highland Wildlife Park and Waltzing Waters.

⊗ Boathouse Restaurant, Loch Insh Watersports

Located in a converted boathouse with views over the loch and Strathspey. Morning coffee and tea, homebaking, snacks, salads, children's menus and evening menus are available. Outside seating. Open March to October, daily 1000–1000.

☕ La Cafètiere, Kingussie

Small café offering a selection of snacks and homebakes. Friendly atmosphere and cyclists welcome. Open Monday to Saturday.

Route description

From the car park at Aviemore railway station, TL onto main road (B9152).

1 Veer left into layby opposite Tourist Information Centre and join track at far end of layby, SP Coylumbridge/Rothiemurchas. Continue on track under railway bridge.

2 TR onto minor road running parallel to river. *0.5km (0.3 miles)*

3 TL and follow track across old bridge, SP Coylumbridge/Rothiemurchas. Continue on track.

4 The fishery is on LHS at end of track. TL and rejoin main road.

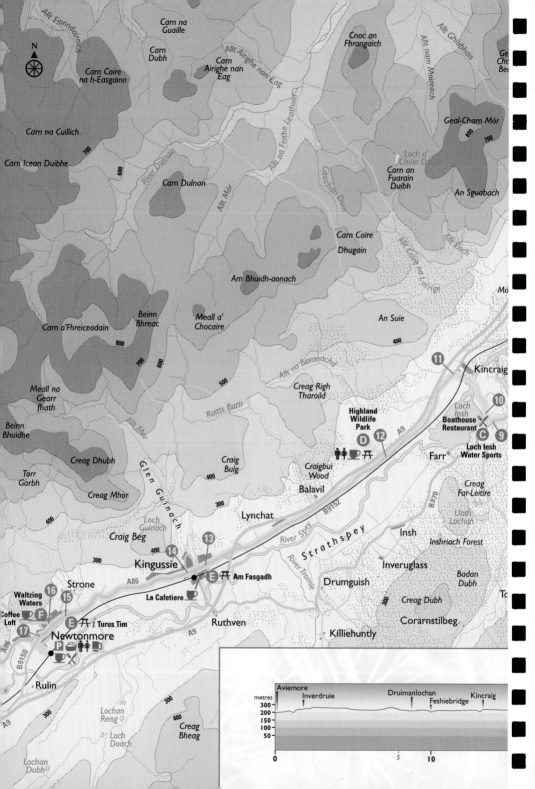

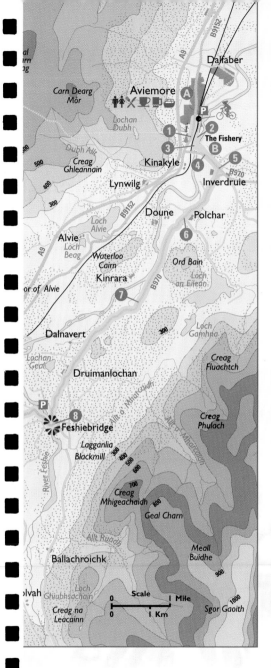

5 TR (with care), SP Inshriach/Feshybridge/Insh B970.

6 SO past access road to Loch an Eilein (on LHS beside monument).

7 Pass Inshriach Nursery on RHS (6km/3.5 miles) and continue on B970.

8 Cross the River Feshie (spectacular views of gorge and river from bridge). Two hundred metres past bridge, on RHS, there is a car park where several walks and off-road cycle routes start.

9 TR, SP Kincraig/Loch Insh Watersports.
11.5km (7 miles)

10 TL to visit Loch Insh Watersports. To continue route, stay on road towards Kincraig.

11 TL at TJ, SP Kingussie (A86).

12 TR (with care) to visit the Highland Wildlife Park (17km/10.5 miles). To continue route, stay on road to Kingussie.

13 To visit Am Fasgadh, TL, SP Highland Folk Museum, for 200m. To continue route, stay on road into Kingussie. *23km (14.5 miles)*

14 To finish route at Kingussie and return to Aviemore by train, TL, SP Station/Ruthven Barracks for 300m and TR into station. To continue route, stay on road towards Newtonmore.

15 To visit Turis Tim, TL just before Newtonmore, SP Highland Folk Museum (26.5km/16.5 miles). To continue route, stay on road into Newtonmore.

16 Pass Waltzing Waters on RHS.

17 TL, SP Perth. Then, TL, SP Station and continue to station to complete the route and return to Aviemore by train.

28.5 km (17.5 miles)

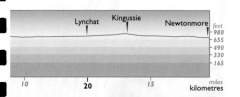

ELGIN, LOSSIEMOUTH AND DUFFUS CASTLE

Route information

Distance 31.5km (19.5 miles)

Grade Easy

Terrain Well-surfaced, quiet and reasonably flat roads, suitable for most cyclists (including older children with road sense) on any type of bicycle.

Time to allow 3–4 hours.

Getting there by car Elgin is on the A96 Aberdeen to Inverness road. Follow SP Perth A941 and then SP for the station, where there is car parking. Alternatively, park beside the library and museum.

Getting there by train Elgin is on the Aberdeen to Inverness line run by Scotrail. There is a frequent service which carries bicycles free – booking is essential. Telephone (0345) 484950 for information.

*This route takes you across the Laigh of Moray, the fertile flat lands to the north of Elgin. Through Elgin the route follows the River Lossie past the spectacular cathedral. Following part of the old Elgin to Lossiemouth railway line, and passing the birthplace of Ramsay MacDonald (the first labour prime minister), the route follows the River Lossie to its mouth beside the harbour. On past West Beach, towards Covesea. The route then follows the perimeter of RAF Lossiemouth and returns to Elgin, finish-*ing *with a tour of Cooper Park, a local favourite with play areas and a biblical garden. Allow extra time to visit the places of interest along the route.*

Places of interest along the route

Ⓐ Elgin

A former Royal Burgh and traditional market town, Elgin is one of the oldest settlements in Scotland. **Elgin Museum**, High Street, was established in 1836 and houses award-winning displays of geology, archeology and social history. Internationally known for its collection of fossilised fish and reptiles, there is also a collection of Pictish stones. Open April to October, Monday–Friday 1000–1700, Saturday 1100–1600, Sunday 1400–1700; November to March by appointment. Charge. Telephone (01343) 543675. **Elgin Cathedral**, North College Street, was built on a site thought to have been occupied since the 6th century. Once known as the Lantern of the North, the cathedral was burned and damaged a number of times, most notably by the Wolf of Badenoch (Alistair Stewart, the outlawed son of King Robert II) who rampaged through the area in 1390. Historic Scotland property. Open April to September, Monday–Saturday 0930–1830, Sunday 1400–1830; October to March, Monday–Saturday 0930–1830, Sunday 1400–1630, closed Thursday afternoon and Friday. Charge. Telephone (01343) 547171. Adjacent to the cathedral, in King Street, is the **Biblical Garden**, 1.2ha (3 acres) planted with every species of plant mentioned in the bible. Open May to September, daily 1000–1930. Admission free. **Johnstons Cashmere**

Mill, Newmill – established for 200 years, the mill is the only one in Britain to convert raw material into the finished product, utilising both traditional and modern techniques. Exhibition, audio-visual presentation, mill tours and coffee shop. Open all year, Monday–Saturday 0900–1730; July to September closes 1800 and also open Sunday 1100–1700. Admission free. Telephone (01343) 554040. **Moray Motor Museum**, Bridge Street, houses an extensive and acclaimed collection of vintage cars and motor cycles in a converted mill. Open April to October, daily 1100–1700. Charge. Telephone (01343) 544933.

B Lossiemouth Fisheries Museum, Lossiemouth

Lossiemouth was the local port and is now a bustling seaside resort. The museum is housed in old net mending sheds in the Pitgaveny Quay Marina complex at Lossiemouth harbour. It is staffed by local volunteers, many of them ex-fishermen who give visitors a first hand insight into the fishing industry. Exhibits have been donated by local families and there is display on Ramsay MacDonald. Open Easter to September, Monday–Saturday 1000–1700. Charge. Telephone (01343) 812326.

C Duffus Castle, near Elgin

The ruins were once the seat of the De Moravia family (the Murrays). The castle's moat is intact and filled with water and a fine 14th-century tower still stands. Historic Scotland property. Open at all reasonable times. Admission free. Telephone 0131 668 8600.

River Lossie, Elgin

Food and drink

There are numerous restaurants, cafés, pubs and convenience stores in Elgin, located close to the Tourist Information Centre and museum. Refreshments are also available at Johnstons Cashmere Mill.

☕ Harbour Antiques & Tearoom, Lossiemouth

Overlooking Pitgaveny Quay Marina, serving breakfasts, snacks, homebakes and lunches. Seating inside and on the quay. Children welcome. Open all year.

☕ Skerry Brae Hotel, Lossiemouth

Coffees, teas, snacks, lunches and full meals, often using locally caught seafood. The lounge bar and veranda offer great views. Seating inside and out. Children welcome.

Route description

Start from car park at Elgin railway station. TR out of car park, onto main road. TL at roundabout (SP blank for left turn). Veer right at corner, following road to right.

1 TL, SP Tourist Information Centre/Museum/Parking. TR at TJ opposite Tourist Information Centre, into High Street.

2 Veer left at market cross (Elgin Museum is on LHS). Continue past museum to back of car park. Follow SP for Library/Cooper Park and walk your bicycle for 100m to cross Elgin ring road. Remount and continue along North College Street (which runs along edge of park).

3 TL at TJ, SP Johnstons Woollen Mill ¹/₄ mile, and cross the River Lossie. Pass Johnstons Woollen Mill on right.

4 TR, SP Pitgaveny 2, Calcots 2, for 100m. Then, TL, SP Pitgaveny.

5 SO at XR, SP Lossiemouth 5, and continue.

6 TL at TJ, SP Lossie B9103/3 miles. Continue on B9103. **4km (2.5 miles)**

7 Continue for 200m past cemetery (on right) and TR onto small track through bushes. Follow track as it descends down a ramp to old railway track, continues through bushes and onto tarmac (10km/6 miles). Cross tarmac road and rejoin track. Pass Ramsay Macdonald's birthplace (SP on right) and Lossiemouth market cross. Rejoin road just before TJ.

11km (7 miles)

8 TR at TJ. To visit Lossiemouth East Beach continue SO for 200m and cross footbridge on LHS. To continue route immediately TL along esplanade.

9 TR at TJ and continue SO past children's play park on RHS, harbour on RHS and Pitgaveny Quay on LHS. Follow road past marina harbour and round corner to commercial harbour.

10 Pass the Bunker (a fisherman's shelter). TL up High Street (12km/7.5miles). SO at XR.

11 TR at XR (beside Bank of Scotland and Clydesdale banks) and continue through Lossiemouth.

12 TR to visit Lossiemouth West Beach, SP West Beach Car Park. Otherwise, cycle SO past golf club and course. Continue out of Lossiemouth on B9040, towards lighthouse. Follow the perimeter of RAF Lossiemouth (watch out for low flying planes).

13 Pass Covesea Riding School on left and Covesea Go Karts/Golf/Putting on right.

16km (10 miles)

14 TL at XR, SP Bike Route 5.

15 To visit Duffus Castle, TR at TJ, SP Bike Route 5 (20.5km/12.5 miles). Continue to TL, SP Duffus Castle, and cycle down track to castle. After visit, retrace along track, TR onto road and continue to direction 16.

Otherwise, to continue route, TL at TJ.

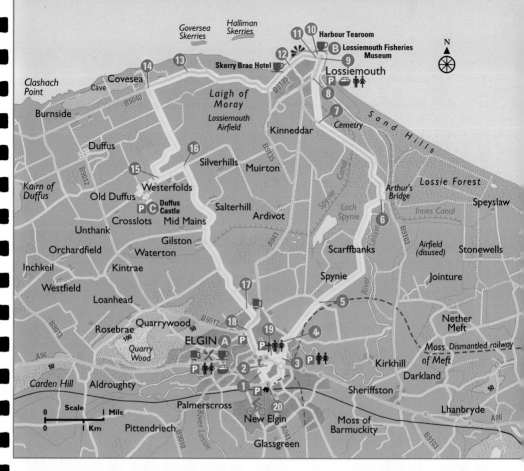

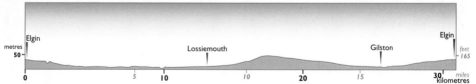

16 TR up minor road with row of houses (before you get to airbase hangers). No SP but there is a Bike Route 2 SP facing the other way when you enter this road (23.5 km/14.5 miles). Continue on this road towards Elgin.

17 SO through mini roundabout. Continue and TR at TJ opposite Bonnie Earl pub, onto main road (A941).

18 TL, SP Moray Motor Museum. Pass museum on RHS after 100m (29km/18 miles). Continue over old bridge and veer left down path. TR onto road and follow it around Cooper Pond, passing library on right, play park on left, Biblical Garden, toilets and bowling green on left.

19 TR at TJ at cathedral. Then TL at XR, SP Bike Route 1, continue alongside cathedral and TL at TJ. SO WITH CARE at roundabout, SP Perth.

20 SO at roundabout, SP Inverness. Then, TL into station car park, SP Station, to complete the route. **31.5km (19.5 miles)**

SPEYSIDE WAY, GLEN RINNES AND ABERLOUR

Route information

Distance   31.5km (19.5 miles)

Grade   Moderate

Terrain   Well-surfaced, minor roads and forestry tracks, suitable for any type of bicycle with low gears to cope with the gradual climbs.

Time to allow   3–4 hours.

Getting there by car   The route starts at Boat of Fiddich car park, Craigellachie: from Elgin, follow A941 SP Perth and take exit SP Keith A95; from Grantown-on-Spey, follow A95 SP Keith/Elgin and take exit SP Keith A95. Pass through Craigellachie and TR, SP Fiddich Park/Speyside Way Visitor Centre (100m before Fiddichside Inn and bridge).

Getting there by train   There is no practical rail access to this ride. The nearest stations are Keith (19km/12 miles) and Elgin (21km/ 13 miles).

This route follows the line of the disused Strathspey railway (now part of the Speyside Way) from Craigellachie to Dufftown. A gradual climb takes you out of Dufftown along Glen Rinnes for a short ascent by Ben Rinnes (at 840m, the highest hill in the area). On along forestry tracks, with spectacular views over the Spey Valley. A steep, fast descent takes you into Aberlour where the route rejoins the Speyside Way to return along the river to Craigellachie, with a short optional diversion to the local cooperage.

Places of interest along the route

Ⓐ Speyside Way Visitor Centre, Boat of Fiddich, Craigellachie
For information on the Speyside Way and its natural history – the Countryside Ranger can provide advice for users of the route. Opening times vary. Admission free. Telephone the ranger on (01340) 881266. For further information on the Speyside Way, see page 8.

Ⓑ Dufftown
Dufftown is the centre of the whisky industry – seven distilleries were constructed here between 1823 and 1898. For details see route 4.

Ⓒ The Village Store, Aberlour
Bought by Mr Affie Macintyre in 1922, run as a general store until 1978, and still perfectly preserved today. Open mid-February to mid-January, Monday–Friday 1000–1700, Sunday 1330–1700. Admission by donation. Telephone (01340) 871243.

Ⓓ Speyside Cooperage, Craigellachie
Discover the ancient craft of coopering, from the acorn to the cask, through audio-visual presentations and a viewing gallery. Also a herd of Highland cattle on site. Gift shop and picnic area. Open all year, Monday–Friday 0930–1630; also June–September, Saturday 0930–1630. Admission charge. Telephone (01340) 871108.

Food and drink

There is plenty of choice in Dufftown.

⊗ Craigellachie Inn, Craigellachie
Traditional hotel overlooking the River Spey, offering a range of meals. Access from the Speyside Way in Craigellachie (200m from Fiddich Park along Tomintoul route).

🍺 Highlander Inn, Craigellachie
Small inn offering snacks, bar meals and an à la carte menu. Food is served in the bar, on the veranda overlooking the River Spey or in the dining room.

⊗ Taste of Speyside, Dufftown
Offering the best of local produce – seafood, venison, steaks and local vegetables.

☕ Old Pantry, Aberlour
Morning coffees and afternoon teas, delicious homebakes, snacks and meals.

Craigellachie Bridge

Route description

Start from Boat of Fiddich car park, Craigellachie. At Speyside Way XR SP, beside toilets, follow track SP Dufftown. Pass playhouse and park area and continue along Speyside Way.

1 Cross River Fiddich over Newton Bridge and continue on track.

2 Follow track through gate, past Convalmore distillery and on to picnic site and car park. **5.5km (3.5 miles)**

3 TL onto main road (A941). Pass the old Keith & District Railway Line on LHS.

4 To visit distillery and castle, TL SP Glenfiddich Distillery/Balvenie Castle. Then, TR to visit distillery or continue for 100m and TR to castle. Retrace to A941 and TL.

To continue route, SO, SP Town Centre 1/2 (and other local SP) and climb into Dufftown

5 TR, SP Tomintoul B9009 (B9008) and continue. **8.5km (5 miles)**

6 TR, SP Edinvillie, and climb.

7 Pass Ben Rinnes car park and viewpoint (15.5km/9.5 miles), then descend.

8 As you descend, look out for house in clearing on RHS. 250m after house, TR up track for 50m and pass through green gate.

9 TL at track junction.

10 Continue under pylons, staying on main track.

11 Keep right on main track (trees cleared to left – great views). **20.5km (12.5 miles)**

12 SO, as big track drops to left.

13 SO, following main track (small track off to right).

14 SO, following main track round bend (small tracks off to right and left).

15 Cross small burn and continue (passing small track to right after 100m).

16 SO, following main track (other track off to left).

17 TL at XR (major track SO and minor track to right).

18 SO, as track joins from left. Continue through gate and descend into clearing at fields.

19 TL at track junction. Follow track as it gradually changes from track to tarmac through trees. Descend. **25km (15.5 miles)**

20 TR at TJ (out of Aldechie Road on hairpin bend) and descend into Aberlour past hospital, tennis courts and bowling green.

21 SO at XR in town centre, SP Car Park/Speyside Way/Alice Little Park (the Village Store is on right hand corner of the small square). Continue into car park.

22 At back of car park, TR onto track SP Speyside Way. Follow track to footbridge where TR and join riverside track, SP Speyside Way. Follow track along River Spey, past children's play area and out of Aberlour travelling downstream – the track is SP with Speyside Way posts. Pass through gates and over slip road beside sewage works.

23 SO through gate. To visit Speyside Cooperage TR up track ramp (just after gate) to main road and:

a SO across main road, SP Bluehill Quarry/Camping.

b LHF (RHF goes to campsite). Pass quarry on RHS.

c TL at TJ.

d TL into Speyside Cooperage. After visit, TL back into road and descend into Craigellachie.

e Pass Craigellachie Distillery on RHS, then TR, SP Primary School/Village Hall. Follow road over hill and along Leslie Terrace.

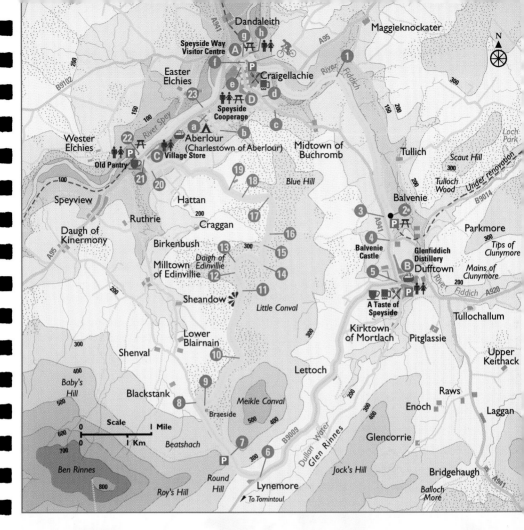

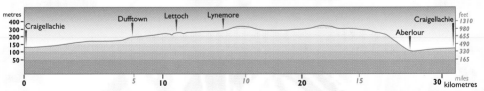

f TL at TJ and descend.

g TR at TJ onto main road (SP up hill for primary school/village hall).

h TR, SP Fiddich Park/Speyside Way Visitor Centre and finish the ride in the car park.

Otherwise, continue through old railway tunnel, past children's play area on LHS. Pass Speyside Way Visitor Centre (on LHS through gate) to complete route in car park.

31.5km (19.5 miles)

THE BLACK ISLE – FORTROSE AND CROMARTY

Route information

Distance 38.5km (24 miles)

Grade Moderate

Terrain Well-surfaced, quiet roads, with some gradual climbs – suitable for any type of bicycle and all cyclists, including older children who can cope with the distance and climbs.

Time to allow 3–4 hours.

Getting there by car Fortrose is on the A832, 14.5km (9 miles) east of the Tore roundabout on the A9. There is parking beside Fortrose Cathedral (off main street, SP Fortrose Cathedral).

Getting there by train There is no practical railway access to this ride. The nearest railway station is at Muir of Ord (24km/15 miles).

This circular route takes you around the tip of the Black Isle peninsula. From Fortrose, through Rosemarkie, up Fairy Glen (home to a black witch!) and onto the Eathie road which climbs along a ridge, an extension of the Great Glen fault line. From the ridge, there are spectacular views over the Moray Firth and the cliffs below are well known for their fossil beds. The route then loops through Cromarty, along the coast of the Cromarty Firth to the village of Jemimaville (named after the Dutch wife of an 18th-century landowner). The Cromarty Firth was an important naval harbour which sheltered convoys heading to Murmansk in Russia. A final climb over the peninsula, and a steep descent with excellent views takes you back to Fortrose.

Route description

From the parking beside Fortrose Cathedral, TL onto road.

1 TR at TJ, onto main street through Fortrose. Continue on this road to Rosemarkie.

2 Cycle through Rosemarkie, passing Groam House Museum on RHS. Continue out of Rosemarkie and climb through Fairy Glen.

3 TR, SP Eathie and Cromarty cycle SP (3km/2 miles). Continue along this road towards Cromarty, with extensive views of the Moray Firth and the Cairngorms.

4 TR at TJ, no SP, onto A832.

14km (8.5 miles)

5 Pass Dolphin Ecosse on RHS. TR, SP Cromarty Courthouse and Hugh Miller's Cottage (both on RHS of Church Street). Retrace route to junction with main road, TR and continue through Cromarty.

6 TL just before parking and follow road round beside coastguard station.

7 TR at end of coastguard station.

8 TL at TJ by Royal Hotel. Continue out of Cromarty and through Jemimaville on B9163.

9 Pass Udale Bay Reserve on RHS.

10 TL, SP Fortrose B9160 (28km/17.5 miles) and continue on this road towards Fortrose.

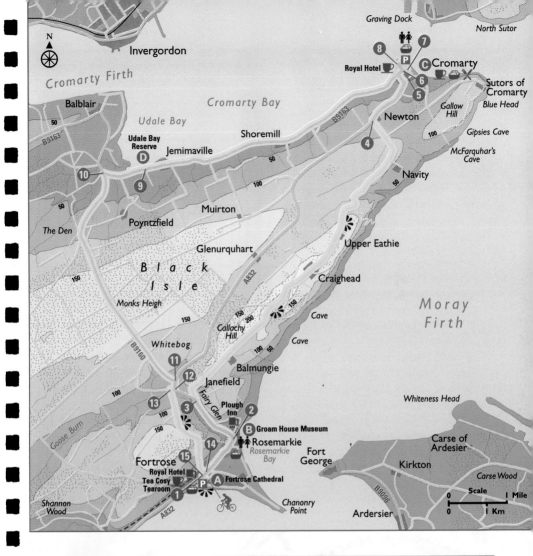

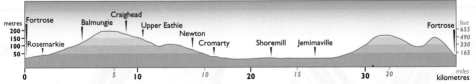

11 TR, SP Fortrose A823. ***35km (21.5 miles)***

12 TR, SP Raddery.

13 TL, no SP. Climb then descend steeply (WITH CARE) into Fortrose – excellent views.

14 TR, no SP, and cycle along main street.

15 TL, SP Fortrose Cathedral and finish the route beside parking on RHS.

38.5km (24 miles)

Places of interest along the route

A Fortrose Cathedral, Fortrose

In the former royal burgh of Fortrose lie the remains of the 14th- and 15th-century cathedral. The cathedral was the burial site of the Mackenzies of Seaforth and the characteristic red sandstone was said to have been removed to build Cromwell's fortress at Inverness. Historic Scotland property. Open April to September, daily 0930–1830. Admission free. Telephone 0131 668 8800.

B Groam House Museum, Rosemarkie

The museum illustrates the history of the Picts and houses the famous Rosemarkie cross-slab – one of the most spectacular pictish carved stones in existence. There are a number of other locally found sculptured stones on display and visitors can make rubbings of the pictish symbols, play a reconstructed Pictish harp, hear the prophecies of the Brahan Seer and see an audio-visual presentation. Open Easter week and May to September, Monday–Saturday 1000–1700, Sunday 1400–1630; October to April, weekends only 1400–1600. Charge. Telephone (01381) 620961.

C Cromarty

Cromarty dates back to at least the 6th century, when a church was founded by a missionary from Iona. Cromarty was largely bypassed by modern road and rail links and remains a fine example of an 18th-century town. **Cromarty Courthouse**, Church Street, is a community run museum which uses the latest technology to explore the town's history. Open Easter to October, daily 1000–1700. Telephone (01381) 600418 for further details and to confirm winter opening. **Hugh Miller's Cottage**, Church Street, was the home of the renowned stonemason, geologist, church reformer, journalist and

Food and drink

There are restaurants, cafés, pubs and convenience stores in Cromarty.

Tea Cosy Tearoom, Fortrose
Teas, coffees, light refreshments and lunches.

Royal Hotel, Fortrose
Traditional hotel serving bar meals and snacks, daily 1200–1400 and 1730–2100.

Plough Inn, Rosemarkie
Bar meals served daily 1200–1400 and 1730–2100.

author. The cottage is full of personal effects, including Miller's geologist hammer, microscope and a beautiful fossil collection. A video film charts his achievements. National Trust for Scotland property. Open May to September, Monday–Saturday 1100–1300 and 1400–1700. Charge. Telephone (01381) 600245. **Dolphin Ecosse** operate daily boat trips to see the most northerly group of bottlenose dolphins in the world. Trips take place all year round, weather permitting, but advance booking is essential. Telephone (01381) 600323 for further information.

D Udale Bay Reserve, Jemimaville

The RSPB's Udale Bay Reserve is an extensive area of mudflats, saltmarshes and wet grassland on the Cromarty Firth. The reserve supports a large wildfowl and wading bird population, which is best visited at high tide. In late summer visitors can often see ospreys fishing; in autumn around 5000 widgeons arrive to feed on the eel grass growing in the area. There is a birdwatching hide. Reserve open all year, at all reasonable times. Admission free. Telephone (01463) 715000.

CARRBRIDGE TO GRANTOWN-ON-SPEY

Route information

Distance 40km (25 miles)

Grade Easy

Terrain Well-surfaced roads, quiet and gently undulating, suitable for any type of bicycle. A short section of the route (1km/0.6 mile) uses the A95 which is narrow and can be busy (although it is part of the National Cycle Route – NCR7). The route is suitable for older children with good road sense and who can cycle the distance.

Time to allow 4 hours.

Getting there by car Carrbridge is 11.5km (7 miles) north of Aviemore. Leave the A9 and follow SP for Carrbridge (B9152). The route starts from the car park in the centre of the village, SP Toilets/Car Park.

Getting there by train Carrbridge station (no parking) is on the Glasgow/Edinburgh/Perth/Inverness line run by Scotrail. There is a frequent service which carries bicycles free of charge – booking is essential. Telephone (0345) 484950 for information. To reach the start of the route, leave the station along the exit road. TR at TJ, and descend into the village. TR at TJ in Carrbridge – the start is at the car park 100m on the LHS of the road. At the end of the ride, retrace to the station. Starting from Carrbridge station adds 2.5km (1.5 miles) to the total route distance.

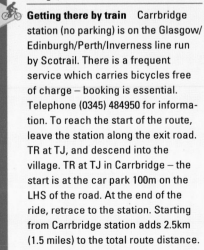

From Carrbridge, with its well-known 18th-century bridge, following the River Dulnain to Dulnain Bridge, where the Dulnain joins the River Spey. There are spectacular views of the River Dulnain, the Spey Valley and the Monadhliath Mountains on this relatively flat section of route. The route crosses the River Spey at Grantown-on-Spey and climbs to the 6070.5ha (15,000 acre) Revack Estate. The return route follows the undulating, western bank of the River Spey, through the villages of Nethy Bridge (at the centre of the Abernethy Forest) and Boat of Garten (home of the Strathspey Steam Railway). The route joins NCR7 at Boat of Garten for a gradual climb and descent back to Carrbridge. Allow extra time to visit Revack Estate and Landmark Forest Heritage Park.

Places of interest along the route

Ⓐ Grantown-on-Spey

The town was constructed by the Laird of Grant from 1766, as a focus for new manufacturing industry. The arrival of the railway coincided with the Victorians' enthusiasm for Scotland, and the Highlands in particular. **Revack** was a shooting lodge built in the 1860s. Today this traditional Highland estate has diversified and offers the visitor a range of activities – there are wildlife trails through the estate, nesting sites for several different species of birds, orchids, a walled garden, ornamental lakes and stocked fishing. Also children's adventure playground, gift shop, tearoom, restaurant and picnic area. Open all year (except Christmas and New Year), daily 1000–1730. Admission free. Telephone (01479) 872234.

B Strathspey Steam Railway, Boat of Garten

Strathspey Steam Railway runs steam and diesel trains the 8.5km (5 miles) between Boat of Garten and Aviemore. See route 5 for further information.

C Landmark Forest Heritage Centre, Carrbridge

The centre offers a vast range of activities and an insight into the history of the area and the forest. Also Wild Water Coaster, adventure areas and a treetop trail. Restaurant and snack bar. Open all year (except Christmas Day), 0930–1800 (closes 2000 July and August, 1700 in winter). Charge. Telephone 0800 7313446 or (01479) 841613.

Route description

Start at the car park in Carrbridge, on the main street SP Toilets/Car Park. TL out of car park, onto main road.

1   TL into Carr Road, opposite Carrbridge Village Hall, and continue towards A95.

2   TR up fork to A95, SP Dulnain Bridge 1¹/₄ miles/A938.   **8.5km (5 miles)**

3   TR at TJ, onto A95. Descend, following river into Dulnain Bridge.

4   Continue SO through Dulnain Bridge.
                                    10.5km (6.5 miles)

5   Pass view point/picnic area on LHS of road.

6   TL through gate onto old road, 20m before junction with main A95 road (11km/7 miles).

7   TL at end of old road and rejoin main A95 road WITH CARE. Pass Craggan Mill Restaurant (LHS) and Fishery (RHS).

8   TL 100m past Craggan Mill. Veer right through gate and back onto old road (which runs parallel to new A95).

9   TL at end of old road, SP Grantown-on-Spey – Capital of Strathspey. Continue into Grantown-on-Spey.

Food and drink

Plenty of choice in Grantown-on-Spey. Refreshments are available at Revack Estate and Landmark Forest Heritage Centre.

☕ Old Bakery Tearoom and Coffee Shop, Carrbridge

Offering home baking, soups, snacks and meals. Cyclists welcome. Open all year.

✕ Craggan Mill Restaurant, Grantown-on-Spey

British and Italian cooking. Families welcome. Open all year.

☕ Pollyanna's Tearoom, Nethybridge

Homebakes, snacks and meals. Cyclists welcome. Open end February to end October, Tuesday–Sunday (closed Monday).

🍽 Boat Hotel, Boat of Garten

Hotel and lounge bar serving lunches 1215–1415, evening meals 1800–2100.

10   TR at traffic lights, SP Elgin A95/A941/Tomintoul/A939.   **15.5km (9.5 miles)**

11   SO at roundabout, SP Elgin A941/Keith A95.

12   TR WITH CARE, SP Revack Estate/Nethybridge/Coylumbridge B970. Pass Strathaird Spey Valley Smokehouse on RHS after turn (visitors welcome).

13   To visit Revack Estate, TL, SP Revack Estate, into estate and climb to visitor centre. On leaving estate, descend to main entrance, TL onto B970 and continue route.

14   Pass Roy Castle ruins on RHS.
                                    23km (14.5 miles)

15   SO through Nethybridge, continuing on B970.

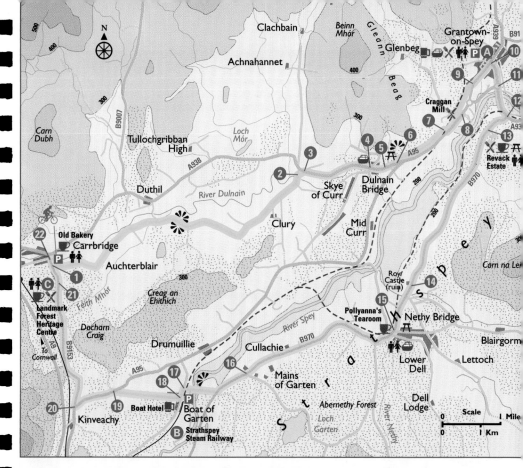

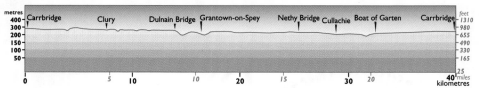

16 TR, SP Boat of Garten ³/₄, and join NCR7. Cross River Spey (tremendous views to west over Cairngorm mountains).

30.5km (19 miles)

17 Follow road as it swings to left and continue into Boat of Garten.

18 To visit Strathspey Steam Railway, TL just beside Boat Hotel. Following visit, TL out of station and rejoin road through Boat of Garten. On leaving village, join track which runs parallel to road.

19 TL at TJ, SP Perth/Inverness/A9/A95 (34.5 km/21.5 miles). TAKE CARE – this 1km (0.6 mile) section is narrow and can be busy.

20 TR at TJ, SP Carrbridge, following NCR7.

21 Pass Landmark Forest Heritage Centre on LHS and descend into Carrbridge.

39.5 km (24.5 miles)

22 TR into car park, SP Toilets/Car Park to complete the ride. ***40km (25 miles)***

49

INVERNESS, GLEN CONVINTH AND A LOCH NESS CRUISE

Route information

 Distance 41.5km (26 miles)

Grade Strenuous

Terrain Well-surfaced, generally quiet roads, and a small section of canal towpath, suitable for any type of bicycle with low gears – there are a number of steep climbs. The route is suitable for experienced cyclists and older children with good road sense and the ability to cope with the hilly terrain. The 3km (2 mile) section between Drumnadrochit and Urquhart Castle is on a busy section of the A82 and is not suitable for younger children or inexperienced cyclists.

Time to allow 3–4 hours.

Getting there by car Inverness is reached from the A9, A96 and A82. There is plenty of parking in the town and beside the railway station.

Getting there by train Inverness is at the hub of rail services from Aberdeen, Wick and Thurso, Kyle of Lochalsh and the south. Telephone (0345) 484950 for further information.

From Inverness, the route follows the banks of the River Ness, the Caledonian Canal and the Beauly Firth, before a climb over the Aird hills, and a descent into undulating Glen Convinth.

On to Drumnadrochit – home to various Loch Ness Monster (Nessie) attractions – before the route heads south along the shores of Loch Ness to Urquhart Castle. The return journey is made by boat to avoid using the busy A82 – Jacobite Cruises sail from Urquhart Castle, through Loch Ness and the Caledonian Canal to Inverness. You will have the opportunity to spot Nessie and admire the beautiful scenery. The cruises operate from Easter to October, with regular daily sailings. Bicycles must be booked in advance. Telephone (01463) 233999. Allow extra time to visit the attractions at Drumnadrochit.

Places of interest along the route

A Inverness

Inverness is the main administrative centre of the Highlands. **Inverness Museum and Art Gallery**, Castle Wynd, contains a variety of displays including archaeology, art, natural and local history, Highland silver, weapons and musical instruments. Restaurant. Open all year, Monday–Saturday 0900–1700. Admission free. Telephone (01463) 237114. At **Inverness Garrison**, Inverness Castle, visitors are recruited to the castle's garrison and are given a tour of the facilities and an insight into the life of recruits in 1745, just before the Jacobite uprising. Open all year, daily 1030–1730. Charge. Telephone (01463) 243363. **Bught Park** houses a sports centre, Aquadome, minigolf, ice rink and access to river walks. Also in the park is **Bught Floral Hall**, a climatically controlled environment housing a sub-tropical landscape, waterfalls, fountains, ferns, orchids and tropical fish. Coffee shop. Open April to September, Monday–Friday 1000–2000, weekends 1000–1800; October to March, daily 1000–dusk. Admission to park free but charge for activities and Bught Floral Hall. Telephone (01643) 222755. Other attractions in Inverness are the **Scottish Kiltmaker** and **Dolphin Cruises** (see route 14) and **Holm Mill** (see route 22).

Ⓑ Drumnadrochit

Drumnadrochit sits by the side of the largest bay on Loch Ness. The **Official Loch Ness Monster Exhibition**, Drumnadrochit Hotel, has a multi-media presentation on highland folklore, pre-history Scotland, Loch Ness exploration and, of course, the Loch Ness Monster. Coffee shop and restaurant in hotel. Open Easter–October at 0930, closing times vary; winter 1000–1600. Charge. Telephone (01456) 450573. **Drum Farm**, Village Green, is a working livestock farm with feeding area, playbarns and lots of opportunities to meet the animals. Tearoom and picnic area. Open Easter to October, Monday–Saturday 1000–1630 (July and August open until 1800). Charge. Telephone (01456) 450788.

Ⓒ Urquhart Castle, Strone Point

The ruined remains of one of Scotland's largest castles. Originally thought to have been built in the 13th century by the Lord of the Isles, the castle was owned by the Grant family in the 16th century. In 1652 the castle was blown up to avoid it becoming a Jacobite stronghold. Many sightings of the Loch Ness Monster have been made from the castle. Open April to September, daily 0930–1830; October to March, daily 0930–1630. Charge. Telephone (01456) 450551.

The route also passes **Highland Aromatic** in Drumchardine and **Moniack Winery** at Moniack Castle – see route 14 for details.

(see route 14) and **Holm Mill** (see route 22).

Food and drink

Plenty of choice in Inverness. There is a coffee shop and restaurant at Drumnadrochit Hotel and a tearoom at Drum Farm.

Bog Roy Inn, Inchmore
Traditional inn (renowned for smuggling), serving snacks and bar meals daily 1200–1400 and 1800–2030.

Route description

From the main entrance of Inverness railway station, SO across main road and down Union Street (one way street). TL at TJ, into Church Street and walk across the 20m of pedestrian precinct.

1 TR onto Bridge Street (opposite the Tourist Information Centre – Inverness Museum/Art Gallery and Garrison are behind TIC). TL at traffic lights and continue parallel to River Ness along Castle Road.

2 TR and follow road next to river.

3 TR and walk across footbridge, SP No Cycling. TL after bridge and continue parallel to River Ness, passing Bught Park.

4 Arrive TJ. Cross road and TL towards canal bridge. TR immediately before bridge and follow canal towpath. Pass canal locks.

5 TL at TJ to rejoin road and cross canal bridge (5km/3 miles). SO at roundabout, past Muirton Hotel, SP Beauly/Dingwall A862. Follow cycle lane out of Inverness. Pass Ardfern Nursery on LHS (10.5km/6.5 miles) and Northern Lights Candle workshop on LHS (11.5km/7 miles) and continue along A862.

6 Pass Highland Aromatics on LHS.
15 km (9.5 miles)

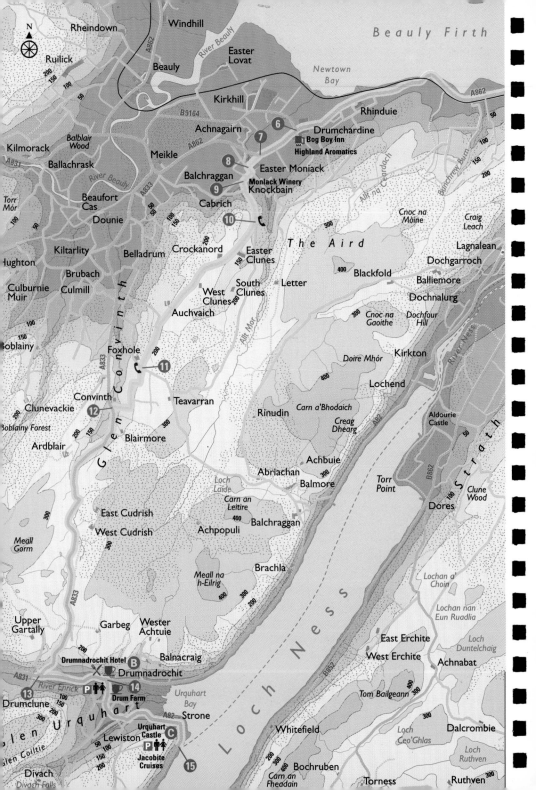

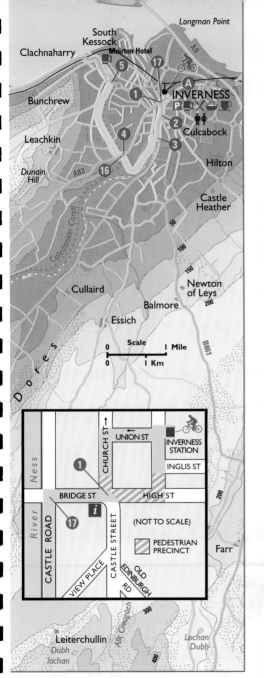

7 TL, SP Easter Moniack Farm only (yellow SP). Continue over closed bridge and TL at TJ just after bridge.

8 Keep right, SP Moniack Winery/Cabrich/Clunes. Pass Moniack winery on RHS.
16.5km (10.5 miles)

9 TL, SP Knockbain/Clunes. Continue and pass telephone box on LHS.

10 Just after telephone box, keep right on road and continue.

11 TL at TJ (beside old school and telephone box) for 30m. Then, TR for descent.
23km (14.5 miles)

12 TL at TJ (after descent), and join A833. Continue towards Drumnadrochit.

13 TL at TJ onto A82, SP Drumnadrochit.

14 TR at TJ in Drumnadrochit, SP Fort William A82 (36km/22.5 miles). The Loch Ness Monster Exhibition (Drumnadrochit Hotel) is on LHS of junction. Pass Drum Farm on LHS. Continue, with care, on busy A82 to Urquhart Castle.

15 Arrive Urquhart Castle and Jacobite Cruises, for return to Inverness.
38.5km (24 miles)

16 Arrive Inverness. Leave Jacobite Cruises reception area, TR and cross canal bridge. TR into Bught Road. Retrace route back alongside River Ness into Inverness via footbridge.

17 TR at traffic lights, into Bridge Street. Pass Tourist Information Centre and walk SO up pedestrianised High Street. TL into Inlgis Street and TL into Academy Street. TR, SP Station, to finish route. *41.5km (26 miles)*

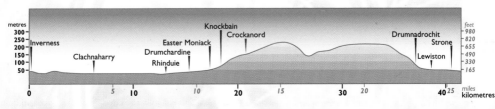

TOMINTOUL, GLENLIVET AND A'AN SIDE

Route information

 Distance   43km (27 miles)

Grade   Strenuous

Terrain   Well-surfaced roads, forestry and mountain tracks. The route involves some steep climbs and rough, and often muddy, tracks and is, therefore, suitable only for experienced cyclists on mountain bikes. Part of the track is on exposed mountain moorland and cyclists should be suitably prepared for changes in the weather, which can occur rapidly. Take adequate warm, weatherproof clothing, sturdy footwear, food and drink. This route should only be followed in good weather.

Time to allow   4–6 hours.

Getting there by car   Tomintoul is on the A939 Grantown-on-Spey to Braemar road. There is parking in the village square, in a car park just off the main street, and at the Glenlivet Estate Office/Information Centre at the top (southern) end of the village.

 Getting there by train   There is no practical rail access to this route. Aviemore and Carrbridge are the nearest railway stations, both approximately 32km (20 miles) away.

This adventurous route takes you through the spectacular Glenlivet Estate following the Conglass and Livet Waters and the River Avon (A'an), reaching a height of 570m (295 feet) at the top of Carn Daimh. Starting in Tomintoul, the route descends following the Conglass Water. Using a designated cycle route (Glenlivet Estate Bike Route 3) the route climbs through Glenconglass, the forest and over open moorland to the top of Carn Daimh. There are spectacular views over the Cairngorm, Ladder and Cromdale Hills and the surrounding glens. After a rapid, bumpy and sometimes muddy descent, the route follows the River Livet to Drumin. At Drumin the route turns and follows the beautiful River Avon upstream through A'an side, crossing on one of the foot/swing bridges (Glenlivet Estate Bike Route 1/2). The route continues along the eastern bank of the River Avon to Bridge of Avon for a gradual climb back to Tomintoul. Allow extra time to visit the places of interest along the route.

Places of interest along the route

Ⓐ Tomintoul

Tomintoul is one of the highest villages in Scotland. Lying between the Ladder and Cromdale Hills, at the edge of the Cairngorms, **Glenlivet Crown Estate** encompasses over 752 square km (90 square miles) of diverse countryside. The estate provides opportunities for outdoor sports. A ranger service at the estate office provides advice on activities and leaflets with cycle trail and walk information. This is a working estate with extensive farming, fishing and field sports. Care should be taken to comply with any restrictions in place and to keep to the designated cycle routes. The estate is open all year, although access is restricted during the lambing and stalking seasons. Admission free. Telephone (01807) 580283 for further information. **Tomintoul Museum** features a reconstructed crofter's kitchen and smiddy with displays describing the story of Tomintoul and Glenlivet. Open April, May and October, Monday–Friday 1000–1600; July and August, Monday–Saturday 1000–1630; September, Monday–Saturday 1000–1600. Admission free. Telephone (01309) 673701.

Ⓑ Glenlivet Distillery, Glenlivet

Originally built in 1824 and relocated further down the hill in 1858, the distillery has had an interesting and turbulent history which visitors can discover while touring the stills. Coffee shop. Open mid March to end October, Monday–Saturday 1000–1600, Sunday 1230–1600; July and August open daily until 1800. Charge. Telephone (01542) 783220. Blairfindy Castle (opposite the distillery) was built in 1586 by the Earl of Huntly. There is no public access

Food and drink

There is a village shop in Tomnavoulin and a coffee shop at Glenlivet Distillery.

Ⓧ **Clockhouse Restaurant, Tomintoul**
Serving breakfasts, snacks and meals.

Ⓓ **Glen Avon Hotel, Tomintoul**
Hotel with cozy, open fire. Bar meals served daily 1200–1430 and 1730–2000.

to the castle due to its dangerous condition, but it can be viewed from the road.

Ⓒ Museum of Scottish Country Life, Drumin

The museum contains farming implements, journals, records, household items and a vast collection of country curios. The 14th-century Drumin Castle, which can be seen from the museum, was a stronghold of the Wolf of Badenoch, who razed the towns of Forres and Elgin. Open in summer, daily 1030–1730. Charge.

Glenlivet

Route description

Start from Glenlivet Estate Office/Information Centre. TR out of car park and descend towards village centre.

1 TR, SP Braemar A939/Dufftown B9008.

2 TL, SP Croughly.

3 TR, small SP for Glenconglass car park/Carn Daimh.

4 Pass house on LHS and TL into car park. Continue on tarmac through gate (5km/3 miles). SO (as tarmac drops to right) and pass through another gate.

5 SO towards farm (as track drops to right).

6 SO (as track goes to left), SP Bikes 2/3.

7 TR, SP Bike 3.

8 TL, SP Bike 3. Then, SO and climb, SP Bike 3 (50m later). (TR goes through metal gate, TL starts to descend.)

9 TR onto a less used track, SP Bike 3 (10km/6 miles). Continue to climb through trees (height in metres SP every so often). Track comes out of trees and climbs to cairn at top of Carn Daimh – the last 400m is over open moorland on a rough, steep track.

10 Cross style and follow track which runs SO, past cairn, SP Bike 3. Descend on a rough track over open moorland.

11 TR, SP Bike 3, through wooden gate into forest, SP Glenlivet Estate.

12 TL at TJ, SP Tomnavoulin. Continue on this track out of forest, through three fields (using gates to pass between fields) and down to ford.

13 Cross ford and continue on track, crossing a second ford and passing in front of a farm. *16km (10 miles)*

14 SO (as track joins from left), and descend into Tomnavoulin. *19km (12 miles)*

15 Arrive Tomnavoulin (the village shop is 50m on RHS). TL at TJ and cross bridge, SP Bike 3.

16 TL, just after house on LHS, small/discreet SP Woodland Walk/Bike 3 (20km/12.5 miles). Pass woodland walks on LHS as you climb.

17 To visit Glenlivet Distillery, TR for 300m.

Or, SO to continue route.

18 TL at TJ, beside Drumin Smithy. *25km (15.5 miles)*

19 Pass Museum of Scottish Country Life and Drumin Castle on RHS and continue.

20 TR, SP Fodderletter 4, and cross metal bridge (30.5km/19 miles). Pass Inverlochy Farm (LHS, name on barn), then large barns on RHS.

21 TL to cross River Avon (A'an) on foot/swing bridge, SP Bike 1/2. *35.5km (22 miles)*

22 TL off the bridge, follow field fence for 100m and TR (before row of trees) to strike up hill. At top of hill, go through gate in fence.

23 TR and rejoin tarmac road (TL is SP Bike 1/2). Pass the Soldier Stone on RHS (information plaque) and the old Bridge of Avon on RHS (a military bridge built in 1754, now a local picnic site).

24 TL at TJ by telephone box, SP Tomintoul A939 (39.5km/24.5 miles). Climb into Tomintoul. Pass Tourist Information Centre on RHS of village square. Arrive at the Glenlivet Estate Office and Information Centre to complete the route. *43km (27 miles)*

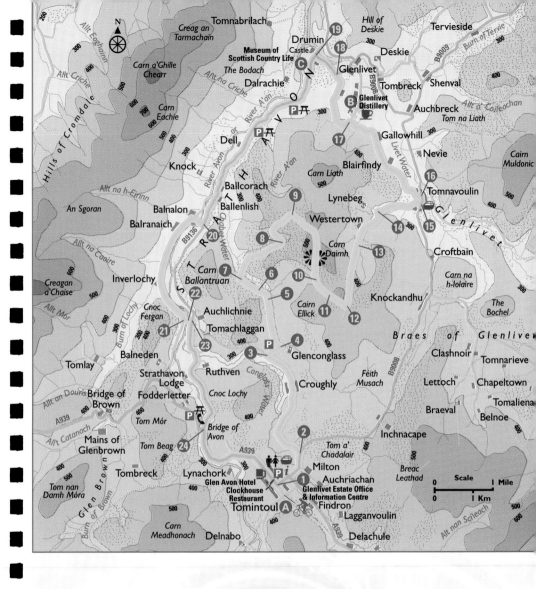

N

Tomnabrilach
Creag an Tarmachain
Hill of Deskie
Tervieside
Burn of Tervie
B9009

Drumin
Museum of Scottish Country Life
Castle
Deskie
Glenlivet
The Bodach
Dalrachie
Tombreck
Shenval
Auchbreck
Tom na Liath
Allt a' Coileachan

Carn a'Ghille Chearr
Carn Eachie
Glenlivet Distillery
Gallowhill
Nevie
Cairn Muldonic

Dell
Knock
Blairfindy
Carn Liath
Tomnavoulin
Glenlivet

An Sgoran
Balnalon
Ballcorach
Ballenlish
Lynebeg
Westertown
Croftbain

Balranaich
Carn Daimh
Carn na h-Iolaire
The Bochel

Creagan a'Chaise
Inverlochy
Carn Ballantruan
Cairn Ellick
Knockandhu
Braes of Glenlivet

Gnoc Fergan
Auchlichnie
Tomachlaggan
Glenconglass
Clashnoir
Tomnarieve
Lettoch
Chapeltown

Tomlay
Balneden
Ruthven
Croughly
Féith Musach
Braeval
Tomaliena
Belnoe

Bridge of Brown
Strathavon Lodge
Fodderletter
Cnoc Lochy
Bridge of Avon
Inchnacape

Mains of Glenbrown
Tom Mór
Tom Beag
Tom a' Chadalair
Breac Leathad
Scale
1 Mile
1 Km

Tombreck
Lynachork
Glen Avon Hotel
Clockhouse Restaurant
Milton
Auchriachan
Tomintoul
Glenlivet Estate Office & Information Centre
Findron
Lagganvoulin

Tom nan Damh Móra
Carn Meadhonach
Delnabo
Delachule

Hills of Cromdale

S T R A T H A V O N

Glenlivet

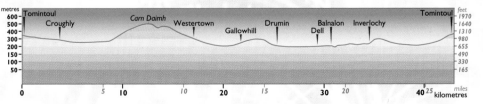

metres
600
500
400
300
200
150
100
50

Tomintoul
Croughly
Carn Daimh
Westertown
Gallowhill
Drumin
Balnalon
Dell
Inverlochy
Tomintoul

feet
1970
1640
1310
980
655
490
330
165

0   5   10   15   20   25
kilometres
miles

BEAULY FIRTH CIRCUIT

Route information

 Distance 46.5km (29 miles)

Grade Easy

 Terrain Well-surfaced roads, suitable for any type of bicycle. There is one long climb. The road out of Inverness can be busy and the route is, therefore, more suitable for experienced cyclists.

Time to allow 4 hours.

 Getting there by car Inverness is reached from the A9, A96 and A82. There is plenty of parking in the town and beside the railway station.

Getting there by train Inverness is at the hub of rail services from Aberdeen, Wick and Thurso, Kyle of Lochalsh and the south. Telephone (0345) 484950 for timetable information.

From Inverness, across the River Ness and the Caledonian Canal to join the relatively flat road that skirts the southern shore of the Beauly Firth. There are glorious views over the firth towards the northern Highlands. The route climbs from the firth and descends past Reelig Glen, through Clan Fraser country. Crossing the River Beauly at Lovat Bridge, the route loops through Beauly to Muir of Ord. A local cycle route is followed from Muir of Ord to the northern shore of the Beauly Firth, near Redcastle. A picturesque cycle along the coast and through North Kessock takes you to Kessock Bridge, with excellent views down the Moray Firth and the Beauly Firth. From here, the route descends back into Inverness. Allow extra time to visit the numerous attractions.

Places of interest along the route

A Inverness

Inverness is the main adminsitrative centre of the Highlands and has much to offer visitors. The **Scottish Kiltmaker Visitor Centre**, Huntly Street, illustrates the history and craft of the kilt. Open mid-May to end September, Monday–Saturday 0900–2100, Sunday 1000–1700. Admission free. Telephone (01463) 222781. **Dolphin Cruises**, passed on the way back into Inverness, offers wildlife cruises in the Beauly Firth and Moray Firth on M.V. *Miss Serenity*. Visitors can see the common and grey seals, porpoises, Minke whales, terns, gannets, razorbills, kittiwakes, and ospreys. Regular daily sailings between March and October. Charge. Telephone (01463) 717900. See also routes 12, 22 and 25.

B Reelig Glen

A small, picturesque glen containing over 200 varieties of plants, splendid walks and a tree spotters trail. The glen was developed and laid out by James Baillie Fraser (1783–1856) in the style of Capability Brown. Forestry Commission property. Open at all reasonable times.

C Moniack Winery, Moniack Castle

The winery produces Scottish country wines, liqueurs and preserves in the castle, built in 1580 by the Frasers. A guided tour explains the wine-making process, from fermentation to bottling. Also audio-visual presentation explaining the business and the history of Clan Fraser, and tasting sessions. Open March to October, Monday–Saturday 1000–1700; November to February, Monday–Saturday 1100–1600. Charge. Telephone (01463) 831283.

D Highland Aromatics, Drumchardine

Located in a former church, Highland Aromatics produces hand-finished soaps which incorporate specially blended Highland perfumes. Visitors welcome. Open all year, Monday to Friday 1000–1600. Admission free. Telephone (01463) 831625.

E Beauly

Standing near the mouth of the River Beauly, in Clan Fraser country, the town was originally laid out in 1840 by Thomas Fraser of Strichen. The monument in the town's square commemorates the Lovat Scouts who served in the Boer War. Beauly has extensive floral displays which do consistently well in the Scotland in Bloom and Britain in Bloom competitions. There are also countryside and river walks. **Beauly Priory** was founded by the Carthusian monks (the Valliscaulians) from Burgundy in 1230, and today only the ruins remain. Beside the priory are monuments and graves to the Chisholms,

Frasers and Mackenzies of Kintail. Historic Scotland property. Open April to September, Monday–Saturday 0930–1830, Sunday 0930–1830. Charge. Telephone 0131 668 8800. **Made in Scotland** is a unique craft outlet where visitors can watch crafts people at work (art, knitwear, jewellery, accessories, cushions, candles and pottery). The restaurant offers traditional Scottish food. Open all year, Monday–Saturday 0900–1730, Sunday 1000– 1700. Admission free. Telephone (01463) 782821.

F North Kessock

North Kessock sits facing the narrows between the Beauly Firth and the Moray Firth. There are two wildlife exhibitions – **Dolphin and Seals of the Moray Firth** and the **Red Kite Viewing Centre**. See route 3 for further information.

Food and drink

There is plenty of choice in Inverness, with restaurants, cafés, pubs and convenience stores.

Bog Roy Inn, Inchmore
Traditional inn (once renowned for smuggling), serving bar meals and snacks daily 1200–1400 and 1800–2030.

Beauly Coffee Shop, Beauly
Wide selection of snacks and meals. Open Monday–Saturday 0900–1700.

Kessock Hotel, North Kessock
Hotel serving a range of snacks and meals with veranda seating overlooking the Beauly Firth. The hotel also runs boat trips to view the seals and dolphins.

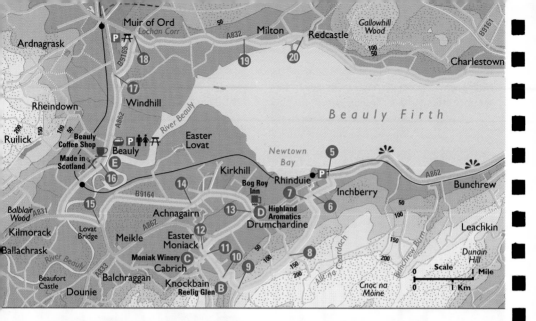

Route description

From the main entrance of Inverness railway station, SO across main road and down Union Street (a one way street). TL at TJ into Church Street and walk across the 20m of pedestrian precinct.

1 TR into Bridge Street (opposite Tourist Information Centre – Inverness Museum/Art Gallery and castle are behind TIC). SO at traffic lights across River Ness. The Kiltmaker Visitor Centre is on the right hand corner, immediately after river.

2 TR with care into Kenneth Street, SP Beauly A862/Aberdeen/Wick A9.

3 SO at Telford Street roundabout, SP A862 Beauly/Moray Firth Tourist Route. SO through next roundabout, SP Beauly A862. Cross canal bridge.

4 SO at roundabout past Muirton Hotel, SP Beauly/Dingwall A862. Follow cycle lane out of Inverness. Pass Ardfern Nursery on LHS (7.5km/4.5 miles), then Northern Lights Candle workshop on LHS (8.5km/5 miles) and continue.

5 TL, SP Inchberry.

6 TL at TJ (give way on bend).

10.5km (6.5 miles)

7 TL and climb (SO goes through gate posts).

8 TL at TJ, and immediately TR (SO is SP dead end). Descend steeply.

9 TR at TJ (TL is SP dead end).

10 Pass Reelig Glen walks and picnic area on LHS (after steep descent).

15km (9.5 miles)

11 To visit Moniack Wineries, TL at TJ (give way) and continue for 200m. After visit, retrace

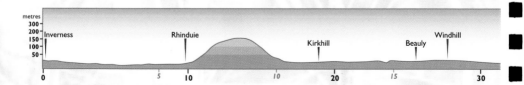

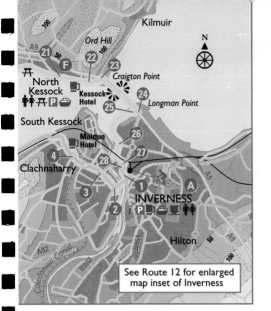

See Route 12 for enlarged
map inset of Inverness

to junction and follow road round to left.
Otherwise, continue SO.

12 TR over bridge, SP road closed. Then TR onto main road (A862).

13 Pass Highland Aromatics on RHS. Then TL, SP Kirkhill B9164. Continue through Kirkhill.

14 Keep right, SP Beauly 3¾ miles, and continue on B9164.

15 TR at TJ, SP Beauly A862. Continue on this road over River Beauly and into Beauly village. **23km (14.5 miles)**

16 Pass Made in Scotland on LHS, then Beauly Priory on RHS. Continue out of Beauly on A862. **26km (16 miles)**

17 TR with care, SP Fortrose/Cromarty B9169.

18 TR at TJ, SP Fortrose and Cromarty A832. **30km (18.5 miles)**

19 TR, SP Redcastle/Charleston and North Kessock/Inverness cycle SP.

20 TR at TJ, no SP, and descend to follow coast round to Charleston and North Kessock. **34.5km (21.5 miles)**

21 TR at TJ, Kessock Bridge/Inverness cycle SP (42km/26 miles). Continue through North Kessock.

22 TL, Kessock Bridge/Inverness cycle SP, and climb up Old Craigton Road, a steep narrow lane. Keep left beside houses.

23 TR and follow cycle lane across Kessock Bridge.

24 TR down ramp, Inverness cycle SP (44km/27.5 miles). Continue through barrier and TR onto road.

25 TL at TJ and follow road which runs parallel to Beauly Firth. Pass Clock Tower on LHS – this marks the site of Cromwell's Inverness Citadel, built in 1652 and demolished in 1661 when the monarchy was restored.

26 SO at traffic lights (meeting point for Dolphin Cruises on RHS by river). Continue under railway bridge. Then TL up Innes Street and continue through the underpass.

27 TR after the underpass, into Rose Street. TL at traffic lights and continue SO through car park and down small lane.

28 TL onto main road. Then TL into station to complete route. **46.5km (29 miles)**

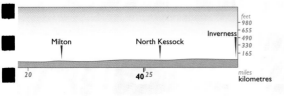

BEAULY AND STRATHGLASS

Route information

Distance 57.5km (35.5 miles)

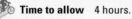

Grade Easy

Terrain Well-surfaced, quiet roads, suitable for all cyclists who can cover the distance, on any type of bicycle.

Time to allow 4 hours.

Getting there by car Beauly is on the A862 Inverness to Dingwall road, part of the Moray Firth Tourist Route. There is parking in the centre of the village, in front of the Priory Hotel.

Getting there by train The nearest railway station is at Muir of Ord, 4km (2.5 miles) away, on the Inverness/Thurso/Wick/Kyle of Lochalsh line run by Scotrail. There is a frequent service and bicycles are carried free of charge – booking is essential. Note that at the time of writing there is no Sunday service. Telephone (0345) 484950 for information. Leave station and TR onto Corry Road. TR at TJ and immediately TR onto main road (A9) through Muir of Ord, SP Moray Firth Coastal Route. Continue on A9 from Muir of Ord to Beauly. This adds 8km (5 miles) to total distance.

The ride starts in Beauly, at the mouth of the River Beauly. Following the western bank of the River Beauly south west, as it meanders through the heart of Clan Chisholm country, the route crosses the River Struy into Strathglass, a picturesque glen. On to Cannich, at the entrance to Glen Affric and Glen Cannich, and across the River Glass. The route now follows the quieter eastern bank of the Rivers Glass and Beauly, passing through Eskadale, the burial place of the Lovats – the other principal clan of the area – before returning to Beauly.

Places of interest along the route

A Beauly

Standing near the mouth of the Beauly River, in Clan Fraser country, the town was originally laid out in 1840 by Thomas Fraser of Strichen. Beauly has extensive floral displays which do consistently well in the Scotland in Bloom and Britain in Bloom competitions. For further information, see route 14.

B Strathfarrar

Strathfarrar runs west from Struy, the point at which the Rivers Farrar and Glass merge to form the River Beauly. The glen, a national nature reserve, is a wildlife haven famed for its deer and golden eagles, and there are ongoing projects to regenerate the ancient Caledonian pine forest. Cyclists a have right of way and can pass the locked gate to enjoy up to 48km (30 miles) of traffic free cycling.

ⓒ Strathglass

Strathglass is a beautiful glen featuring open fields, wooden glens and the drama of the Aigas gorge. In the glen is a a falconry centre, deer farm, fish lift and dams. The Clan Chisholm's burial ground is near Struy. The bridge over the river was built by Thomas Telford, who also designed the Caledonian Canal. Timber from Strathglass was used to refurbish and replace the mast on the *Discovery* – the ship which took Scott to the Antarctic.

Below left: *Beauly Priory*
Below right: *Waterfall near Cannich*

Food and drink

Beauly Coffee Shop, Beauly
A wide selection of snacks and meals available. Open Monday–Saturday 0900–1700.

Struy Inn, Struy
Country hotel serving traditional meals 1200–1400 and 1800–2100.

Slaters Arms, Cannich
Meals served daily 0900–2300. Also a wide selection of beers and guest ales.

Glen Affric Hotel, Cannich
Country hotel serving coffee, afternoon and high tea, bar lunches and evening meals. Open daily.

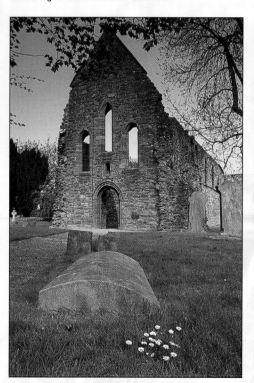

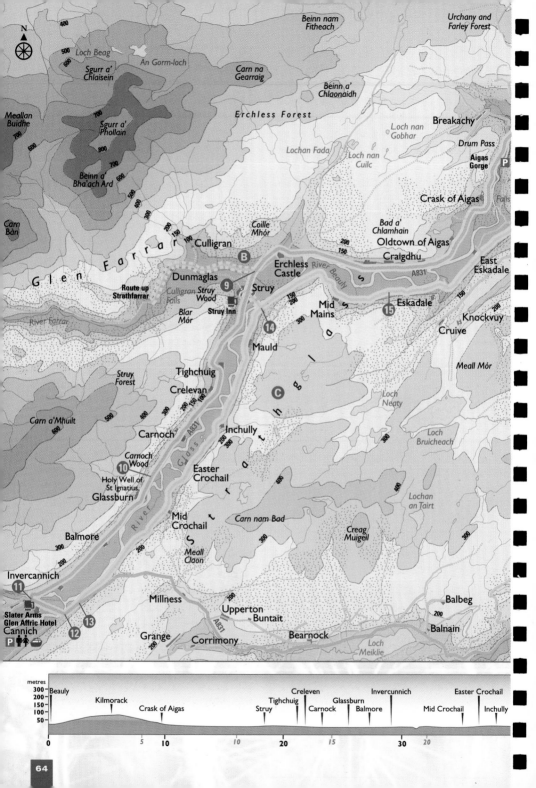

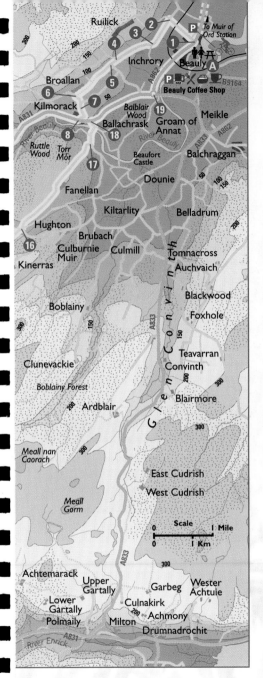

Route description

Start in the centre of Beauly – TL out of car park (next to Priory Hotel), into Beauly main street for 50m.

1 TR beside Bank of Scotland.

2 TL at XR, SP Inchrory.

3 SO under pylons, no SP.

4 Veer left at junction, SP Broallan.

5 SO, SP Broallan.

6 TL at TJ, no SP.   *4.5km (3 miles)*

7 SO, no SP.

8 TR at TJ, no SP, and join main road (A831) towards Cannich (5.5km/3.5 miles). Continue on this road into Struy.

9 TR just before bridge to visit Strathfarrar.

To continue route, SO over Struy Bridge (18km/11 miles) and continue on A831 towards Cannich.

10 Pass the Holy Well of St Ignatius on RHS.   *25km (15.5 miles)*

11 TL, SP Drumnadrochit A831.

12 Veer left, SP Drumnadrochit A831. 30.5km (19 miles)

13 TL, SP Eskadale, and continue on this road, along west side of River Glass.

14 SO at junction, no SP. (TL and cross bridge for Struy Inn.)   *41km (25.5 miles)*

15 Pass gravestone to the oldest deer on LHS and continue.   *44.5km (27.5 miles)*

16 TL, SP Fanellan.   *49.5km (31 miles)*

17 TL, SP Beauly.

18 TR, SP Beauly 2, onto A831.

19 TL, SP Beauly A862 (56km/35 miles). Continue into Beauly and TR into car park by Priory Hotel to finish route.

     57.5km (35.5 miles)

If you started from Muir of Ord, continue SO and retrace your route to the station.

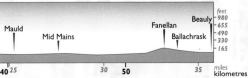

AN SLUGGAN AND RYVOAN PASSES

Route information

Distance   59.5km (37 miles)

Grade   Strenuous

Terrain   Well-surfaced roads, forestry and mountain tracks. There are some steep climbs and rough tracks, suitable only for experienced cyclists on mountain bikes. Part of the route is over exposed mountain moorland and cyclists should be suitably prepared for changes in the weather which can occur rapidly (adequate warm and weatherproof clothing, sturdy footwear, food and drink). This route should only be undertaken in good weather.

Time to allow   4–5 hours. Be aware that during winter, darkness falls quickly and early.

Getting there by car   Aviemore is off the A9 Perth/Inverness road. It is well signposted in both directions. There is a car park beside the railway station and the Tourist Information Centre, both of which are on the main thoroughfare.

Getting there by train   Aviemore is on the Glasgow/Edinburgh/Perth/Inverness line run by Scotrail. There is a frequent service and bicycles are carried free of charge – booking is essential. Telephone (0345) 484950 for information.

One of the classic bicycle routes in this area. From Aviemore, the route follows the Cairngorm ski road to Loch Morlich, from where it turns and climbs the An Sluggan Pass, following an ancient drove rode. A climb and steep descent take you through the forest, and then along minor roads (part of National Cycle Route 7/NCR7), through Boat of Garten, Abernethy forest and Nethy Bridge. The route climbs again and follows another drove road through the forest and over bleak moorland to Ryvoan Pass, from where there are spectacular views of the Cairngorms and Loch Morlich. After a steep, rough descent through Glenmore Forest Park, the route circumnavigates Loch Morlich and follows the ski road back to Aviemore. Allow extra time to visit the attractions.

Food and drink

Plenty of choice in Aviemore. Refreshments are also available at the Fun House and Glenmore Forest Park visitor centre.

Smiddy Coffee Shop, Inverdruie
A woodburning stove and comfy seats. Teas, coffees, homebakes, snacks and lunches available. Cyclists welcome.

Coylumbridge Hotel, Coylumbridge
As well as an American diner, the hotel has a restaurant and carvery.

Boat Hotel, Boat of Garten
Hotel and lounge bar serving lunches 1215–1415 and evening meals 1800–2100.

Pollyanna's Tearoom, Nethy Bridge
Homebakes, snacks and meals. Cyclists welcome. Open end February to end October, Tuesday to Sunday.

Places of interest along the route

Ⓐ Aviemore

Aviemore, once a small Speyside village, is now a major holiday resort catering for skiers and mountaineers in the winter, walkers and cyclists in the summer. See route 1 or 7 for further information.

Ⓑ Rothiemurchus Estate

Rothiemurchus is a working estate, combining farming, forestry and recreation. The estate runs a **fishery** and a **visitor centre** – see route 1 or 7 for details.

Ⓒ Glenmore Forest Park, Glenmore

Glenmore Forest Park is situated in the foothills of the Cairngorm National Nature Reserve, with Loch Morlich as its focal point. The area is a great haven for wildlife, including red and roe deer, pine marten, capercaillie and osprey. The Forestry Commission has a **visitor centre** and there is also the **Cairngorm Reindeer Centre**. See route 1.

The route also passes Coylumbridge Fun House, Strathspey Steam Railway and Loch Garten – see routes 1 and 5.

Route description

Start from Aviemore railway station car park and TL onto main road.

1　Veer left into layby opposite Tourist Information Centre and join track at far end of layby, SP Coylumbridge/Rothiemurchus. Continue on track under railway bridge. TR onto minor road running parallel to river.

2　TL and follow track across old bridge, SP Coylumbridge/Rothiemurchus. Continue to end of track (Rothiemurchus Fishery on LHS), TL and continue along main road.

The Cairngorms and Loch Morlich

3 TL to visit Rothiemurchus Visitor Centre, or SO to continue route.

4 Pass Coylumbridge Hotel and Fun House on LHS. Continue towards Loch Morlich.

5 Arrive Loch Morlich. TL up forestry track (after start of Loch Morlich – opposite car park on RHS of road), SP (10m up track) Public Footpath to Milton of Kincardine.

8km (5 miles)

6 SO across tarmac road.

7 SO at track junction. Climb ahead.

10.5km (6.5 miles)

8 RHF at Y junction near top of climb (LHF climbs to transmitter). Continue through gate beside deer fence.

9 SO through gate (just before farm on RHS). Follow main track.

10 TR at TJ onto tarmac road (B970), no SP (14.5km/9 miles). Continue along this road (part of NCR7).

11 To visit Strathspey Steam Railway, TL, SP Boat of Garten/NCR7. Cross River Spey. Veer left and follow road through Boat of Garten, SP Boat of Garten (20km/12.5 miles). TL to the railway (in front of Boat Hotel). On leaving, TR and retrace route through Boat of Garten and over River Spey.

Otherwise, to continue route, SO, SP Nethy Bridge/Loch Garten B970.

12 TR, SP Loch Garten/Tulloch/Tulloch Moor.

13 Pass Loch Garten forest walks on RHS.

14 TL to visit Loch Garten Osprey Centre. Otherwise, continue SO. *25km (15.5 miles)*

15 Keep left, SP Nethy Bridge.

16 SO at junction, SP Nethy Bridge 2¼.

17 TR at TJ, SP Grantown-on-Spey, and cycle through Nethy Bridge.

18 TR into Dell Road (before bridge beside shop), no SP. *30km (18.5 miles)*

19 SO at road end and follow track, SP Abernethy/Dell Woods Nature Reserve/Glenmore/Braemar.

20 SO at minor junction on LHS.

21 Keep right at minor junction.

22 TL at TJ and climb (SP on tree – no heavy vehicles, also wooden gate and fire beaters at junction). *35.5km (22 miles)*

23 TR through gate and onto track (20m before huts). TL at small XR and start to climb.

24 RHF at junction – LHF drops to ford (38km/23.5 miles). Continue on this main track up through forest and out over moorland. Climb past a small loch and Ryvoan Bothy (on RHS of track at top of the pass). Descend on rough track (take care – walk if necessary) and rejoin good forestry track past Lochan Uaine. Continue, staying on main forestry track.

25 Keep right at track junction and follow yellow/blue posts.

26 Through barrier into car park and back onto tarmac (behind Glenmore Lodge). Continue for climb. *45km (28 miles)*

27 TR onto track at top of hill (just before descent to main road). Follow track in front of Reindeer Centre and Glenmore Forest Park visitor centre. Descend from visitor centre and leave car park. TL onto main road. *46km (28.5 miles)*

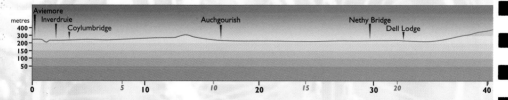

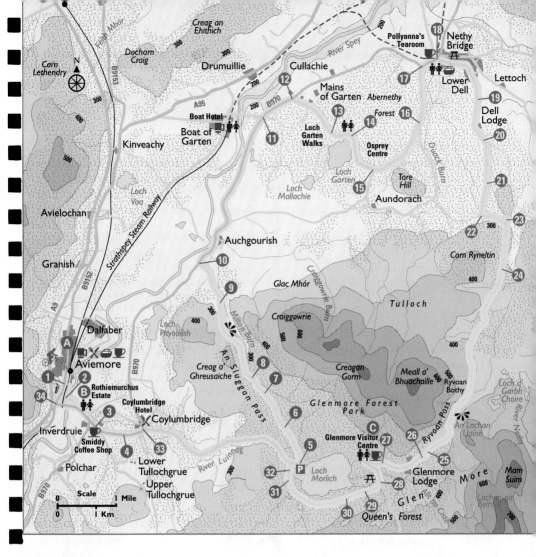

28 TR at snow gates onto track through car park (blue post). Continue and TR at track junction. Follow blue posts.

29 SO at minor junction (where footpath joins from RHS, blue post).

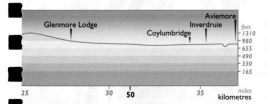

30 TR and descend to gate, through gate and over wooden bridge. Continue.

31 TR at junction onto major forest track.
50km (31 miles)

32 Through gate and over wooden/metal bridge. TL onto tarmac road and continue on road towards Aviemore.

33 SO, SP Aviemore. **55km (34 miles)**

34 TR at TJ, SP Aviemore. TR, SP Station to finish the route. **59.5km (37 miles)**

GLEN FESHIE AND STRATHSPEY – AVIEMORE TO DALWHINNIE

Route information

Distance   65km (40.5 miles)

Grade   Moderate

Terrain   Well-surfaced roads and forestry tracks, suitable for fit cyclists on any type of bicycle (although mountain bikes are preferable). There are some gradual climbs.

Time to allow   4–5 hours.

Getting there by car   Aviemore is off the A9 Perth/Inverness road. It is well signposted in both directions. There is a car park beside the railway station and the Tourist Information Centre, both of which are on the main thoroughfare.

Getting there by train   Aviemore is on the Glasgow/Edinburgh/Perth/Inverness line run by Scotrail. This one-way route returns to Aviemore by train from Kingussie, Newtonmore or Dalwhinnie. There is a frequent service and bicycles are carried free of charge – booking is essential. Telephone (0345) 484950 for information.

A one-way route, starting in Aviemore and gradually climbing through Glen Feshie and the Strathspey floodplain to Dalwhinnie. Out of Aviemore, the route skirts beautiful Loch an Eilein and follows way-marked forestry tracks through Inshriach Forest and across Glen Feshie, from where there are views of the glen, River

Feshie and the distant mountains. The route then joins the National Cycle Route 7 (NCR7) through the villages of Kingussie and Newtonmore, with a final climb to Dalwhinnie. Dalwhinnie, one of the highest villages in Scotland at 362m/1188 feet above sea level, is at the head of the Drumochter Pass and was a stopping off point for Highland cattle drovers on route to the southern markets. The return journey to Aviemore is made by train. Note that the route can be shortened by finishing at either Kingussie station (37.5km/23.5 miles) or Newtonmore station (42.5km/26.5 miles).

Places of interest along the route

Ⓐ Aviemore
Aviemore, once a small Speyside village, is now a major holiday resort catering for skiers and mountaineers in the winter, walkers and cyclists in the summer. Visitors can enjoy a variety of activities. For further information, see route 7.

Ⓑ Kingussie
The RSPB **Insh Marshes Nature Reserve** is one of Scotland's most important areas of flood plain wetland. Nearly 1000 pairs of wading birds breed here during spring and summer, and the marshes are also an important wintering ground for waterfowl. There are hides and nature trails and, during the summmer, organised events. Guided tours April to August, Thursday pm. Picnic area. Open at all times. Admission free. Telephone (01540) 661518. **Ruthven Barracks** are the ruins of an ancient stronghold, rebuilt by General Wade in 1719 as barracks for English soldiers. The barracks were captured and burned by the Jacobite army in 1746. Historic Scotland property.

Access at all times. Admission free. Telephone 0131 668 8800. The **Higland Folk Museum** has two sites, Am Fasgadh in Kingussie and Turus Tim in Newtonmore. See route 7 for details.

ⓒ Dalwhinnie Distillery, Dalwhinnie

Opened in 1898 and the highest distillery in Scotland, Dalwhinnie produces a unique Highland malt whisky. Guided tour, exhibition and shop. Open March to December, Monday–Friday 0930–1630; June to October also Saturday 0930–1630; July and August, also Sunday 1230–1630. Charge. Telephone (01528) 522208.

Also passed is Rothiemurchus Estate, Coylumbridge Fun House and Loch an Eilein (see route 1) and Waltzing Waters (see route 7).

Route description

Start from Aviemore railway station car park and TL onto main road.

1 Veer left into layby opposite Tourist Information Centre and join track at far end of the layby, SP Coylumbridge/Rothiemurchus. Continue on track under railway bridge. TR onto minor road running parallel to river.

2 TL and follow track across old bridge, SP Coylumbridge/Rothiemurchus. Continue to end of track (Rothiemurchus Fishery on LHS), TL and continue along main road.

3 TL to visit Rothiemurchus Visitor Centre, or SO to continue route.

4 Pass Coylumbridge Hotel and the Fun House on LHS.

5 TR, SP Rothiemurchus Caravan Park. Immediately TR up track (do not go into caravan park). Pass through one gate.

6 SO, SP Glen Einich. Continue over style at next gate.

7 SO at junction (5km/3 miles). Continue through one gate and then one deer fence/style.

8 SO at junction.

9 TR at XR, SP Loch an Eilein.

10 TR at Y junction. Continue over two small bridges beside fords.

11 TR, SP Aviemore. Continue through gate and pass red houses. Keep right at minor junction.

12 Through barrier and rejoin tarmac beside car park. For Loch an Eilein Visitor Centre, TL into car park. Otherwise, continue SO for descent.

13 TL at TJ (beside Martineau Monument). *9.5km (6 miles)*

14 Pass Inshriach Nursery on RHS.

15 TL through green metal barrier, up forest track (13km/8 miles). TR and follow SP blue number 2 cycle/ski.

16 TR at TJ, no SP (TL SP blue number 2 cycle/ski). *15km (9.5 miles)*

17 SO past track on LHS (SP blue number 2 cycle/ski).

18 TL at XR, SP Feshiebridge.

19 TR and stay on major track (not SO onto footpath), no SP.

20 Through green barrier and TR onto tarmac road, opposite wooden house.

21 TL at TJ, opposite SP for March House and Glen Feshie Hostel.

22 Cross River Feshie, with great views of river and gorge.

23 TL up small track directly opposite entrance to Feshie Bridge car park, SP yellow number 5 cycle/ski. (The route can be shortened by 7km/4.5 miles here – do not TL but continue SO on tarmac road and rejoin the route at direction 32, where TR.) To continue main route, TL onto forest track and stay on this main track with views to left of Glen Feshie.

24 TL onto narrow track, SP yellow number 5 cycle/ski.

25 TL onto tarmac road by cottage. Continue up Glen Feshie. *20.5km (12.5 miles)*

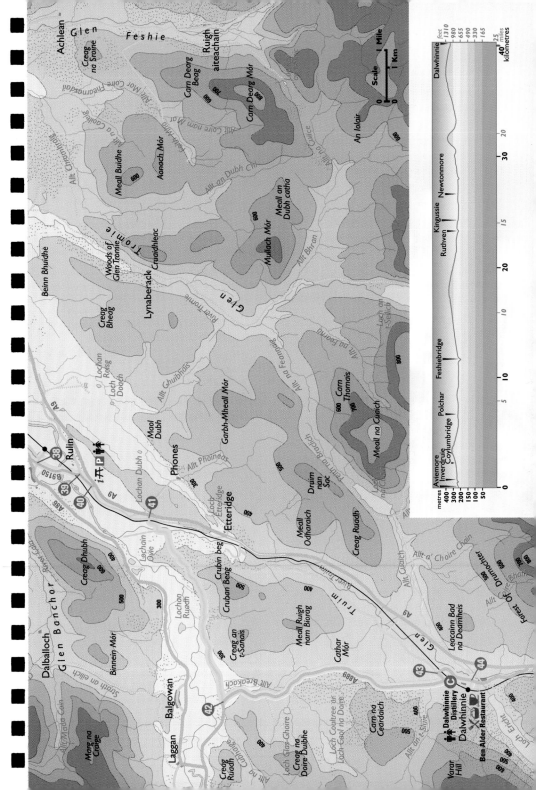

26 TR along farm track, SP Coranstilbeg Farm Road/blue number 4 cycle/ski.

27 TR, SP blue number 4 cycle/ski, and enter forest through green barrier. Start climbing on forest track. Pass quarry on right and descend.

28 TL at TJ, SP blue number 4 cycle/ski (25.5km/16 miles). Continue on main forestry track, SP blue number 4 cycle/ski, past a minor grassy track junction on left.

29 TL at TJ, SP blue number 4 cycle/ski (TR SP Insh). Continue on main forestry track over two footpath XR with cairns and through gate.

30 TR, SP Drumguish (SO SP blue number 4 cycle/ski). Descend through gates into Drumguish. *30km (18.5 miles)*

31 SO at XR in Drumguish village.

32 TL at XR onto road (SO SP no unauthorised access).

33 Pass Insh Marshes Nature Reserve on RHS.

34 Pass Ruthven Barracks on RHS. *35km (21.5 miles)*

35 Continue under main road and over railway line. To finish route in Kingussie, immediately turn into station.

36 For Kingussie, TR at TJ, down main street. To visit the Highland Folk Museum (Am Fasgadh), TR SP Highland Folk Museum.

Otherwise, to continue route, TL at TJ towards Newtonmore.

37 To visit Newtonmore Highland Folk Museum (Turus Tim), TL, SP Highland Folk Museum (41km/25.5 miles). Otherwise, continue SO into Newtonmore. Pass Waltzing Waters on RHS.

38 TL, SP Perth. To finish the route in Newtonmore, TL again, SP Station and follow minor road to station. Otherwise, continue SO.

39 TR, SP Picnic/Information/Toilets. Continue through picnic site to Ralia Information Centre/car park. *44.5km (27.5 miles)*

40 At the far end of the car park there is a one-way slip road from the north carriageway of the A9 into the car park – walk up the right hand verge (against the traffic) for 200m (this avoids cycling on the busy A9 – a section of track will eventually be added here as part of NCR7). TR and join the old road on the RHS of the slip road.

41 TR, SP Glentruim/Laggan. Pass Clan McPherson Memorial on RHS. Continue on this road.

42 TL at TJ, SP (200m before junction) Dalwhinnie. *55km (34 miles)*

43 Keep right at junction, SP Inverness A9, and continue into Dalwhinnie. Pass Dalwhinnie Distillery on RHS.

44 TR, SP Station, for 300m and finish route at Dalwhinnie Station for the return to Aviemore. *65km (40.5 miles)*

Food and drink

There is plenty of choice in Aviemore and Newtonmore. Refreshments are also available at Waltzing Waters.

Smiddy Coffee Shop, Inverdruie
A woodburning stove and comfy seats. Cyclists welcome.

Coylumbridge Hotel, Coylumbridge
As well as an American diner, the hotel has a restaurant and carvery.

La Cafetiere, Kingussie
Homebakes and snacks. Cyclists welcome. Open Monday to Saturday.

Ben Alder Restaurant, Dalwhinnie
On the main road in Dalwhinnie, the restaurant also has a small convenience store.

Route information

Distance 67.5km (42 miles)

Grade Moderate

Terrain Well-surfaced, generally quiet roads, suitable for any type of bicycle, and for all cyclists, including older children who can cope with the distance and a few steep climbs.

Time to allow 4–5 hours.

Getting there by car Inverness is reached from the A9, A96 and A82. There is plenty of parking in town and beside the railway station.

Getting there by train Inverness is at the hub of rail services from Aberdeen, Wick and Thurso, Kyle of Lochalsh and the south. Telephone (0345) 484950 for further information.

Starting from Inverness, the route gradually climbs to the outskirts of the city for a rapid descent to Clava. On, following the River Nairn to Cawdor Castle – the undulating valley road gives spectacular views of Culloden Viaduct and Kilravock Castle. From Cawdor Castle, the route descends to the coastal plains of the Moray Firth, through the village of Ardersier to Fort George. There are spectacular views over the Moray Firth to the Black Isle (you may see dolphins) along this flat section. A gradual climb takes you up through Croy village to Culloden battlefield, for a poignant reminder of the Highlanders who fought for Bonnie Prince Charlie in 1746. A long, gradual descent back into Inverness completes the route. Allow extra time to visit the attractions.

Route description

From main entrance of Inverness railway station, SO across main road and down Union Street (one way street). TL at TJ, into Church Street and walk across the 20m of pedestrian precinct.

1 TL into Castle Street (Inverness Museum/ Art Gallery and Garrison are behind the TIC).

2 Continue SO as road goes right (SP Dores). TL into Old Edinburgh Road, SP Aberdeen/ Perth/Wick. Continue through traffic lights and along Annfield Road.

3 TL at TJ, SP Ullapool/Aberdeen/Perth.

4 TR at mini roundabout, SP Raigmore Hospital/Culloden/Croy.

5 Take second exit (WITH CARE) at large roundabout, SP Culloden/Croy.

6 SO at traffic lights onto B9006, SP Culloden/Croy. Start to climb.

7 TR, WITH CARE, SP Nairnside 1½. Descend. **6.5km (4 miles)**

8 TL at TJ, no SP.

9 Take first TR by row of cottages on LHS, no SP (10km/6 miles). Descend, cross River Nairn and climb.

10 TL at TJ opposite railway arches, no SP. Climb over railway.

11 TL, SP Clava C22, Bike SP 7. Climb. Descend under railway and then climb steeply to pass Clava Cairns on LHS.

12 TR at TJ, no SP (TL Bike SP 7). Continue under railway viaduct and then climb steeply.

13 TL at TJ, no SP, and continue on this road. **15.5km (9.5 miles)**

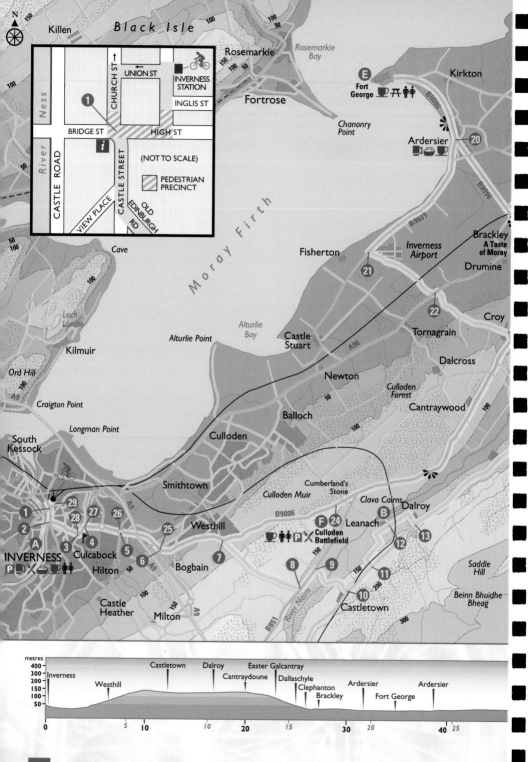

N

Black Isle

Killen
Rosemarkie
Rosemarkie Bay

CHURCH ST
UNION ST
INVERNESS STATION
INGLIS ST
BRIDGE ST
HIGH ST
i
(NOT TO SCALE)
PEDESTRIAN PRECINCT
CASTLE ROAD
CASTLE STREET
VIEW PLACE
OLD EDINBURGH RD

Fortrose

Kirkton
E Fort George

Chanonry Point

Ardersier 20

River Ness

Cave

Moray Firth

Fisherton

Inverness Airport

Brackley
A Taste of Moray
Drumine

B9039

Croy

Loch Lundie

Alturlie Point

Alturlie Bay

Castle Stuart

21

22

Tornagrain

Dalcross

Kilmuir

Ord Hill

Craigton Point

Newton

Culloden Forest

Cantraywood

Longman Point

Culloden

Balloch

South Kessock

Smithtown

Cumberland's Stone

Culloden Muir

Clava Cairns

Dalroy

Westhill

B9006

F 24

Leanach

B Dalroy

29
28 27 26
1
2
A
3
25
Culbock
4
5
6
7
8
9
10
11
12
13

Culloden Battlefield

Saddle Hill

INVERNESS

Culcabock

Hilton

Bogbain

Castletown

Beinn Bhuidhe Bheag

Castle Heather

Milton

River Nairn

metres
400
300
200
150
100
50

Inverness
Westhill
Castletown
Dalroy
Cantraydoune
Easter Galcantray
Dallaschyle
Clephanton
Brackley
Ardersier
Fort George
Ardersier

0   5   10   10   20   15   30   20   40   25

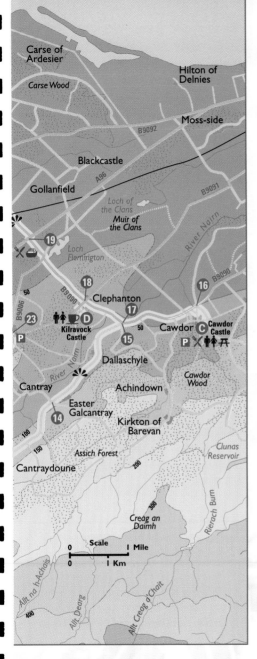

14 SO at XR, SP Cawdor 3.

20km (12.5 miles)

15 TR at TJ, SP Cawdor/Nairn B9090.

16 TR, SP Cawdor Castle (25km/15.5 miles), then TR into castle entrance. Following visit, retrace to entrance and TL. Then, TL at TJ, SP Croy/Culloden.

17 SO, SP Clephanton/Croy/Culloden.

29km (18 miles)

18 To visit Kilravock Castle, TL at XR for 200m, then TL, SP Kilravock Castle. Otherwise, continue SO at XR, SP Fort George.

19 Arrive TJ with busy A96. TR, with care, for 20m, then TL, SP Fort George. Descend.

20 SO through Ardersier, passing viewpoint on LHS (36km/22.5 miles). Continue to Fort George. After visit, retrace route to Ardersier where TR – opposite shops, no SP (42km/ 26 miles). Follow coastal road out of Ardersier towards Inverness Airport.

21 TL, SP Dalcross Industrial Estate/ Inverness Airport. *46.5km (29 miles)*

22 Arrive TJ with busy A96. TL for 50m then TR with care, no SP.

23 TR at TJ in Croy – no SP, by village green (50.5km/31.5miles). TR at TJ, SP Culloden 5/Inverness 10. Continue with views of Culloden Viaduct on LHS. Pass Cumberland's Stone.

24 Pass Culloden Battlefield and Visitor Centre on LHS (58.5km/36.5 miles). Continue – the route is flat for a while and then gradually descends into Inverness.

25 SO at traffic lights, SP Inverness.

26 Take third exit (with care) at large roundabout, SP Town Centre/Raigmore.

27 TL at mini roundabout (65km/40.5 miles). Pass golf course then Kingsmills Hotel on LHS. TR with care up Annfield Road. Continue through traffic lights and onto Old Edinburgh Road.

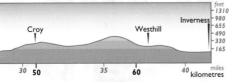

28 TR at TJ and descend past castle. As road swings to left, TR and walk bike through pedestrianised area of High Street.

29 TL and walk bike through pedestrianised area of Inglis Street. TL to join Academy Street. TR, SP Station and finish the route.

67.5km (42 miles)

Places of interest along the route

A Inverness
Inverness is the main adminsitrative centre of the Highlands and has plenty to interest the visitor. See routes 12, 14 and 22 for details.

B Clava Cairns
An extensive group of well-preserved Bronze Age standing stones and cairns. The cairns are thought to be either ancient burial sites or structures for viewing the stars to predict the farming calandar. Historic Scotland property. Access at all reasonable times. Admission free. Telephone 0131 668 8600.

C Cawdor Castle, Cawdor
Cawdor Castle, linked to Shakespeare's *Macbeth,* is one of the most romantic castles in Scotland. Visitors enter the medieval castle via the drawbridge, climb the winding stairs and see the dungeons and the original kitchens. There are beautiful gardens, nature trails, pitch and putt, picnic areas, ponds and riverside walks. Restaurant. Open May to October, daily 1000–1730. Charge. Telephone (01667) 404615.

D Kilravock Castle, Croy
Fifteenth-century castle with extensive grounds containing a large variety of trees, some centuries old. Also nature trails and river. Tearoom. Open April to October, Wednesday 1100–1600. Charge. Telephone (01667) 493258.

E Fort George, near Ardersier
Fort George was built in the aftermath of the Jacobite rebellion of 1745 and the battle of Culloden (1746), as the ultimate defence against further unrest in the Highlands. Costing £1 billion and taking 21 years to complete, this mighty fortification never saw battle. There is an extensive arms and military museum and the regimental museum of the Queen's Own Highlanders. Tearoom and picnic area. Open all year, Monday–Saturday 0930–1830, Sunday 1400–1830 (closed 1630 October to March). Charge. Telephone (01667) 462777.

F Culloden Battlefield, Culloden
On 16 April 1746 the Battle of Culloden was fought on this desolate moorland. Bonnie Prince Charlie hoped to restore the Stuart monarchy but the grossly outnumbered Highland army was crushed by the Duke of Cumberland's men. The Duke of Cumberland surveyed the battle from Cumberland's Stone at the eastern end of the moor. Visitors can walk on the battlefield. Also visitor centre and restaurant. National Trust for Scotland property. Battlefield open at all reasonable times. Visitor centre open April to October, daily 0900–1800; February–March and November–December, daily 1000–1600. Charge. Telephone 01463-790607.

Food and drink

Plenty of choice in Inverness and Ardersier. Refreshments are also available at Cawdor Castle, Kilravock Castle, Fort George and Culloden Visitor Centre.

A Taste of Moray, near Ardersier
Food hall selling traditional local food and restaurant serving snacks and main meals.

SPEYSIDE WAY AND BUCKIE

Route information

 Distance   72km (44.5 miles)

Grade   Moderate

Terrain   Well-surfaced roads, forestry tracks and the Speyside Way. Suitable for any type of bicycle, although sturdy bikes with low gears are preferable – there are some long climbs.

Time to allow   6–8 hours.

Getting there by car   The route starts from Boat of Fiddich car park, Craigellachie – from Elgin, follow A941 SP Perth and take exit SP Keith A95; from Grantown-on-Spey, follow A95 SP Keith/Elgin and take exit SP Keith A95. Pass through Craigellachie and TR, SP Fiddich Park/Speyside Way Visitor Centre (100m before Fiddichside Inn and bridge).

 Getting there by train   There is no practical railway access to this ride. The nearest stations are Keith (19km/ 12 miles) and Elgin (21km/13 miles).

From Craigellachie the route follows the Speyside Way to Spey Bay, using minor roads, forest tracks around Ben Aigan (470m/1542 feet) and traditional fishermens' footpaths. Throughout, there are spectacular views of the River Spey and over the Spey Valley. From Spey Bay the route follows the coast through the fishing village of Portgordon to Buckie, a busy harbour town. The return route climbs from the coast through the Moray countryside

(passing a number of mountain bike trails) back to Craigellachie. Allow extra time for visiting the places of interest. For more information on the Speyside Way see page 8.

Route description

Start from Boat of Fiddich car park, Craigellachie. At Speyside Way XR SP (beside toilets), follow the track SP Speyside Way. TR at TJ, onto road, and cross bridge.

1   TL, SP Arndilly/Speyside Way SP (this is Upper Road). Continue on this road past SP dead end, Arndilly House and Arndilly Home Farm.

2   TR through gate into Ben Aigan Forest, SP Mountain Bike Trails/Speyside Way.

4.5km (3 miles)

3   TL at TJ, SP Speyside Way/red bike SP – blue bike SP points left (5.5 km/3.5 miles). Pass viewpoint and picnic area on LHS.

4   TL, SP Speyside Way, onto a minor track (red bike SP points SO). TAKE CARE – this is a tricky descent and can be slippery.

5   TL at TJ, onto sand track (10km/6 miles). TL at TJ through metal gate, and descend.

6   TL at TJ, SP Speyside Way.

7   TR at TJ, SP Speyside Way (beside Bridgeton Farm). Follow track down in front of farm.

8   TL at TJ, above road and bridge (11.5km/ 7 miles). TR, SP Speyside Way, and follow footpath and steps down to road. TR onto road (beside house).

9   TL beside Boat of Brig car park, SP Speyside Way. Continue under railway bridge and across small metal bridge. Keep right and climb, SP Speyside Way.

N

SPEY BAY

Lossie Forest
Findochty
Portessie
Portessie Bay
Gordonsburgh
Buckie Drifter Museum
Ianstown
Carnoch
Rathven
Connage
Rannas
Hill of Maud
Slate Haugh
Black Hill
Deerhill
Bogside
Buckie
Mains of Buckie
Seatown
Newton of Letterfourie
Whitefield
Addie Hill
Garral Hill
Garralburn
Arthur's Point
Gollachy
Portgordon
Slackend
Slackhead
Walkerdales
Arradoul of Buckie
Drybridge
Oran
Hill of Stonyslacks
Herricks Moss
Burn of Buckie
Mains of Tannachy
Hole
Dryburn
Broadley
Bridge of Tynet
Clochan
Oxhill
Braes of Enzie
Nether Allaloth
Raefin
Croft of Ryeriggs
Ryeriggs
Millstone Hill
Forgie Hill
Burn of Tynet
Spey Bay Hotel
The Links
Spey Bay
Nether Dallachy
Bogmoor
Upper Dallachy
Byres
Auchenhalrig
Newlands
Whiteash Hill Wood
Hill of Fochabers
Leitch's Wood
Fochabers Forest
Whiteash Hill Wood
Gallow Hill
Tugnet
Kingston
Garmouth
Essil
Redhall
Stynie
Mosstodloch
Boghead
Fochabers Folk Museum
Fochabers
Slorach's Wood
Wood of Scotch Ordiequish
Corbiewell
Binns
Tippertait
Finfan
Newton
Connagedale
Hill of Garmouth
New Stynie
Kennieshillock
Marchfield
Bauds
Dipple
Speymouth
Westertown
Ordiequish
Ordiequish Hill
Wood of Ordiequish
Speyslaw
Broomhill
Binn Hill
Stonewells
Waterscott
Muir of Maverston
Maverston
Parkes of Innes
Muir of Lochs
Sleepieshill Wood
Cockeasy
West Bauds
Smithfield
Orbliston
Deanshillock
Culfoldie
Inchberry
Woodside
Nether Meft
Darkland
Urquhart
Lhanbryde
Bogton
Pittensair
Loch Na Bo
Blackburn
Cranloch
Marchfield
Altonside
Woodside
Airfield (disused)
Moss of Meft
Dismantled railway
Innes Canal
Errol
Easter Cotts
Strypes
Greenside

Speymouth
B9015
A96
A990
A942
A98
B9016
B9104
B9103

10 SO, SP Speyside Way (14km/8.5 miles). Continue towards Fochabers.

11 SO to follow road – ignore Speyside Way SP pointing left – (19km/12 miles). Continue on road into Fochabers, passing toilets on RHS.

12 TL at TJ (Fochaber Folk Museum directly opposite), onto main road (A96) through Fochabers. CAUTION – the A96 is busy and cyclists should take care.

13 SO at traffic lights.

14 TL into car park (beside park), SP Crazy Golf/Putting (20.5km/12.5 miles). Continue through car park and follow track that runs down the side of the Water Authority building/enclosure. Follow RHF in track and continue under old and new bridges.

15 TR and cross mound using steps/ramp. Continue on path. TL and join road at Speyside Way information board. Continue.

16 TL off road (Speyside Way SP pointing left up ramp/steps) and veer right to follow river down stream.

17 SO, SP Speyside Way.

18 Pass fishing huts and veer left, SP Speyside Way.

19 TR at junction (moving away from river) for 100m, SP Speyside Way (25km/15.5 miles). TR at next junction SP Speyside Way.

20 SO, SP Speyside Way.

21 SO past old railway embankment, SP Scottish Wildlife Trust. Continue SO (as track goes off to right).

22 TL at TJ with road (in front of houses) for 100m to Tugnet Ice House (SO) and Moray Firth Wildlife Centre (RHS). TR between ice house and wildlife centre. Then TR at TJ from car park onto road. Continue through Spey Bay, passing Spey Bay Hotel on LHS.

23 TL, SP Nether Dallachy. Follow road through village.   *29km (18 miles)*

24 TL, SP Portgordon/Buckie, and continue towards coast.

25 TL at TJ, SP Buckie A990 (35km/21.5 miles). Follow coastal road through Portgordon into Buckie.

26 To visit the Buckie Drifter, continue SO past harbour. TR into Freuchny Road, SP Buckie Drifter. Retrace route alongside harbour and TL, SP Town Centre.

Or, to continue route, TR, SP Town Centre.
41km (25.5 miles)

27 SO at roundabout, no SP, and pass Buckie town centre.

28 SO at A95 XR, SP Drybridge.

29 TR, SP Drybridge.   *45.5km (28.5 miles)*

30 TR at Drybridge (just after river), no SP.

31 TR and immediately TL, no SP.
46.5km (29 miles)

32 SO as road veers to left.

33 TR as road veers to left.

34 SO at XR. Continue through Clochan.

35 TL at XR onto B9106, no SP.
50.5km (31.5 miles)

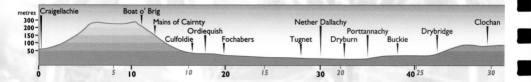

36 TR, old SP for XR/Mulben Boharm/ Craigellachie (54.5km/34 miles). Pass access point for mountain bike trails on RHS.

37 TR and immediately TL, SP Mulben – CAUTION as you cross the busy A96. Pass access point for mountain bike trails on RHS.

38 SO at XR onto A95, SP Craigellachie. Pass access point for mountain bike trails on RHS.

39 TR, SP Belnagarrow, and continue on this road. *65km (40.5 miles)*

40 TR, no SP. Descend, following A95. Pass Fiddichside Inn on LHS. Cross River Fiddich and continue for 100m. *70.5km (44 miles)*

41 TL into the car park, SP Speyside Way, to complete the route. *72km (44.5 miles)*

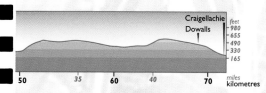

Food and drink

Fochabers and Buckie have restaurants, cafés, pubs and convenience stores.

Ⓧ **Craigellachie Inn, Craigellachie**
Overlooking the River Spey, offering a range of meals. Access from the Speyside Way in Craigellachie (200m from Fiddich Park along Tomintoul route).

Highlander Inn, Craigellachie
Snacks, bar meals and an a la carte menu. Food is served in the bar, on the veranda overlooking the River Spey or in the dining room.

Spey Bay Hotel, Spey Bay
A variety of refreshments available throughout the day.

Places of interest along the route

Ⓐ **Speyside Way Visitor Centre, Boat of Fiddich, Craigellachie**
For information on the Speyside Way and its natural history – the Countryside Ranger can provide advice for users of the route. Opening times vary. Admission free. Telephone the ranger on (01340) 881266 for information.

Ⓑ **Fochabers Folk Museum, Fochabers**
The museum illustrates the history of Fochabers over the past 200 years and includes a large collection of horse drawn carts. Gift shop. Open all year, summer 0930–1300 and 1400–1800; winter closes 1700. Admission free. Telephone (01343) 821204.

Ⓒ **Spey Bay**
Tugnet, at Spey Bay, has been a fishing station for centuries, where salmon are still fished by both the local residents and by ospreys. See route 2 for further information.

Ⓓ **Buckie**
The town of Buckie comprises several fishing villages that grew up along the coast during the 17th, 18th and 19th centuries. The **Buckie Drifter**, Freuchny Road, tells the story of the herring and the fishing communities. There are specially recreated quays, archive footage of steam drifters at work, tours of the harbour and of a RNLI lifeboat. Restaurant. Open April to October, Monday–Saturday 1000–1800, Sunday 1200–1800. Charge. Telephone (01542) 834646. The *Benbola* offers **Wildlife Cruises and Sea Angling**, giving visitors the opportunity to see the local coastline and its wildlife. The cruise can be linked with a wildlife talk at the Moray Firth Wildlife Centre (see route 2). Charge. Sailing times vary depending on the tides and weather. Telephone (01542) 832289 for information.

Craigellachie
Dowalls

feet
-980
-655
-490
-330
-165

50   35   60   40   70   miles
                                kilometres

20 ELGIN, BURGHEAD BAY AND FORRES

Route information

Distance 73km (45.5 miles)

Grade Easy

Terrain Well-surfaced roads and forestry tracks. Suitable for experienced cyclists and older children who can cope with the distance and the one steep climb, on sturdy touring bikes or mountain bikes.

Time to allow 5–6 hours.

Getting there by car Elgin is on the A96 Aberdeen to Inverness road. To reach the start of the route, follow SP Perth A94, then SP station. There is parking at the station and beside the library and museum.

Getting there by train Elgin is on the Aberdeen to Inverness line run by Scotrail. There is a frequent service and bicycles are carried free of charge – booking is essential. Telephone (0345) 484950 for information.

This route starts from Elgin, leaving the town via Cooper Park. On across the Laigh of Moray, past the old Pictish village of Burghead and around Burghead Bay, following tracks through Roseisle Forest. The route continues through Kinloss to Findhorn, from where there are spectacular views over Findhorn Bay and the Moray Firth. Back through Kinloss and into Forres, renowned for its spectacular floral displays. A gradual climb takes you past Dallas Dhu distillery, for a

further steep climb up to Califer viewpoint – the spectacular views over the Moray Firth and Findhorn Bay make up for the effort. Using forestry tracks, a final climb crosses Heldon Hill before the route descends, following the Black Burn back into Elgin. Allow extra time to visit the attractions along the route route.

Places of interest along the route

A Elgin

A former Royal Burgh and traditional market town, Elgin is one of the oldest settlements in Scotland. See route 8 for information.

B Duffus Castle, near Elgin

Ruinous castle with moat intact and full of water. See route 8 for details.

C Burghead

Burghead is one of the oldest coastal villages in Moray. It was an important Pictish settlement and the remains of an ancient fort can still be seen. The Burghead well, a chamber cut into rock surrounding a pool, can be entered. The village performs the ancient custom of Burning the Clavie on 11 January each year (Old Yule Night) when a tar filled barrel is set alight and rolled down Dorrie Hill to ward off evil spirits.

D Findhorn

Findhorn Nature Reserve has a public bird hide and picnic area, with views over Findhorn Bay. Open all year, daily. Admission free. Contact the ranger for further information on (01343) 563469. The **Findhorn Foundation** is a community offering an insight into sustainable living. Visitors can explore the Ecological Village (houses constructed from old whisky vats with grassed roofs, reed water and sewage filtration systems and extensive farming). Admission free. Open all year, daily. Telephone (01309) 690311. **Findhorn Heritage Centre** is an independently run museum, focusing on the history and ecology of Findhorn village. There are a variety of displays, including a salmon fisher's bothy. Open May to September, weekends 1400–1700; June to August also Wednesday–Friday 1400–1700. Charge. Telephone (01309) 690659.

Ⓔ Forres

The ancient town of Forres is the main setting of Shakespeare's *Macbeth*. Today the town offers much to interest the visitor. **Dallas Dhu Distillery** was built in 1898. Although no longer in production, visitors can see how the whisky was produced and the malting area, mash tuns and whisky still. Also whisky sampling. Picnic area. Open April to September, Monday–Saturday 0930–1830, Sunday 1400–1830 (closes 1630 on Sunday, October to March, when also shut on Thursday and Friday). Charge. Telephone (01309) 676548. See route 6 for further information on Forres.

Ⓕ Pluscarden Abbey, near Elgin

A monastery was originally founded here in 1230, and continued until the suppression of monastic life in Scotland in 1560. The buildings fell into ruins until 1948, when a group of Benedictine monks from Prinknash Abbey started restoration. Visitor centre and garden. Open daily, 0445–2045. Admission free. Telephone (01343) 890257.

Food and drink

Plenty of choice in Elgin and Forres.

🅿 **Duffus Inn, Duffus**
Serves a range of bar meals, specialising in steaks. Garden.

🅿 **Red Craig Hotel, Burghead**
Snacks and meals on offer. Views over the Moray Firth.

Route description

Start From Elgin railway station car park and TR onto main road. TL at roundabout (SP blank for this exit). Follow road as it swings to right.

1 TL, SP Tourist Information Centre/Museum/Car Park. TR at TJ, opposite Tourist Information Centre.

2 Veer left past Elgin Museum to the back of car park. Continue SO down North College Street, following SP for pedestrians/Cooper Park to cross (with care) busy Elgin ring road.

3 TL before Elgin Cathedral then TL into Cooper Park (opposite cathedral entrance), Bike SP 1. Follow road past bowling club, library and around pond.

4 Cycle through car park, TL up small track and veer right over old bridge.

5 Pass Moray Motor Museum on LHS.

6 TR at TJ onto main road (A941) and continue around right hand bend.

7 After bend, veer left off A941, over path to road which runs parallel to A941.

8 TR at TJ, and immediately TL at TJ (beside post box and telephone box).   ***3km (2 miles)***

9 SO at mini roundabout and continue along this road.

10 TL at TJ, opposite airfield.

11 Pass Duffus Castle on LHS.

12 Arrive junction with B9012 and TR (no SP, but SP back the way for Duffus Castle). Continue.

13 Follow road round to left.

14 TL at TJ onto B9040, SP Hopeman/Burghead (14km/8.5 miles). Continue through Hopeman, making a detour down Harbour Street on RHS if you wish to visit harbour, beach and ice house. Continue through Cummingston.

N

Moray Firth

Burghead
Harbour

C
15
B9012
Red Craig Hotel
Clarkly Hill
17
18
16
19
20
B9013
21
22
B9089
College of Roseisle
23

Burghead Bay

Roseisle Forest
24
Easter Coltfield

Hempriggs
Coltfield
Kirkton

Findhorn
D
Harbour

Findhorn Foundation
Airfield

Muirhead
Miltonhill

Culbin Forest

Findhorn Bay

Nature Reserve
25
B9011

Kinloss

Abbey
Alves Wood

ellhill

Invererne
B9011
Grange Hall
Mains of Burgie
Toreduff
Dykeside

Kintessack
Moy House
Springfield
26
Monaughty

High Wood
27
28
35
37
38
Heldon Wood
39

ke
29
Forres
34
Burgie Wood
50
100
150
200
40

A96
E
Califer
36
41
B9010

30
Newton of Dalvey
33
Blervie Castle (ruins)
Tulloch

31
Dallas Dhu Distillery
Rafford
32
Muir of Granary

Loch of Blairs
50

Scale
0 ——— 1 Mile
0 ——— 1 Km

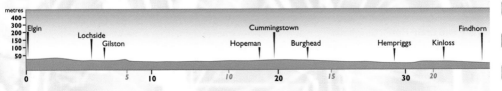

metres
400
300
200
150
100
50

Elgin
Lochside
Gilston
Hopeman
Cummingstown
Burghead
Hempriggs
Kinloss
Findhorn

0   5   10   10   20   15   30   20

Clashach
Point
Covesea
Cave
North
Greens
Stotfield
Branderburgh
Lossiemouth

Burnside
B9040
Airfield
Kinneddar
B9103

Hopeman
Duffus
Inn
(13)
(14)
Cummingstown
Duffus
Westerfolds
(10)
Silverhills
Muirton
Cocklehill
Easter
Greens
Oakenhead

Sand Hills

Kairn of
Duffus
(11)
Balormie
Lossie
Forest

Bank of
Roseisle
(12)
P
B
Duffus
Castle
Broomhill
Old Duffus
Salterhill
Ardivot
Arthurs's
Bridge
Innes Cana

Roseisle
Unthank
Mid
Mains
Scarffbanks
Airfield
(disused)

Bridgend
Orchardfield
Waterton
Gilston
Laigh of
Lochside
Moray
Spynie
Loch
Spynie

Buthill
Inchkeil
Kintrae
Findrassie
Jointure

Westfield
Standingstone
Rosehaugh
Loanhead
(9)
(8)
Linksfield
Dismantled railway
Nether
Meft

Inchstelly
Ardgye
Rosebrae
Quarrywood
Quarry
Wood
50
100
B9012
(7)
(5)
(6)
A
ELGIN
(4)
P
(3)
(2)
Kirkhill
Moss
of Meft

Carden Hill
Aldroughty
A96
(1)
P
Sheriffston
Darkland
Lhanbryde

Cloves
Whitefield
Croft
Redhill
(43)
(44)
(45)
New
Elgin
P
Linkwood
Moss of
Barmuckity
Coxtontower
B9103

Mosstowie
Whitefield
(42)
Pittendriech
Glassgreen
Greens of
Coxton
Errol
50

Hillside
Miltonduff
Birkenhill
Croft
Duffushillock
Easter Cotts
Mains of
Cotts

Forest
150
Muir of
Miltonduff
Heldonside
Nether
Birnie
Riach
Clackmarras
Thornhill
Ordhill
100

Heldon
Hill
200
Torrieston
50
Forester-
seat
Colddach
Auchtertyre
Hillhead
Paddockhaugh
50
Longmorn
Whitewreath
Greenside
150

F
Pluscarden
Abbey
Croy
Upper
Manbeen
Thomshill
Fogwatt
200

Barnhill
P
100
Inchallon
Greens
of Bogside
Upper
Bogside
Easterton
Burnbank
Humbrack

Rosehill
150
Crofts
of Buinach
Wardend
100
Dismantled railway
300

Easter
Kellas
200
Clashconnachie
Leanoch
150
Shongle
Gedloch
200

feet
1310
980
655
490
330
165

Califer
Rafford
Elgin
Pittendriech
Forres

40
25
30
50
35
60
40
70
45
miles
kilometres

87

15 TR, opposite transmitters, SP Burghead.

16 TR at TJ, and continue into Burghead.

17 To visit Burghead, SO. Otherwise, TL, SP Caravan Park/Esplanade/Car Park. Then SO at XR, along Bridge Street.

18 TL and follow tarmac road through caravan park to forest (20km/12.5 miles). Enter forest via track with barrier. Follow main forest track (as lots of small footpaths go off to right and left). The track becomes narrow and sandy beside the dunes, but improves as it re-enters forest.

19 SO at junctions as tracks go off to left and then right.

20 RHF to continue along main track.

21 Follow main track as it swings round to left (small track goes off to right at corner).

22 As main track swings to left, TR onto older/smaller track (which is very straight). Continue through barrier, car park, picnic area and past toilets.

23 TL before next barrier (onto tarmac then track) and leave forest.

24 TR at XR, beside SP Roseisle Forestry Commission (25km/15.5 miles). Continue on this road into Kinloss.

25 Arrive Kinloss. Pass abbey on LHS. To visit Findhorn, TR, with care, SP Findhorn/Findhorn Foundation (31km/19 miles). Follow the road to Findhorn passing nature reserve on LHS, Findhorn Foundation on RHS and Findhorn Heritage Centre in village. Retrace from Findhorn to Kinloss.

Otherwise, to continue route, SO through Kinloss, SP Forres.

26 SO at roundabout, SP Forres.

27 Pass SP Seunos Stone on RHS.

28 Pass Grant Park (access to Nelson Tower), SP Car Park/Toilets/Nelson Tower.

Continue through Forres, passing Falconer Museum on LHS.

29 TL at roundabout, SP Grantown A940.

30 TL, SP Dallas Dhu Distillery.
44km (27.5 miles)

31 Pass Dallas Dhu Distillery on LHS.

32 TL at TJ, SP Forres B9010 (opposite telephone box).

33 TR on brow of hill (beside war memorial). Pass ruins of Blervie Castle on LHS.

34 TR at XR (no SP, but bike SP 3 back the way), and climb windy road (48.5km/30 miles). At top of climb pass Califer Braes viewpoint and picnic area on LHS.

35 TR, SP Pluscarden.

36 TL into first metal gated forestry track (55.5km/34.5 miles) and pass three tracks (one to left, one to right, then one to left).

37 TR onto track and continue on this main track as it climbs (past small track to left and one to right).

38 TL at TJ for 100m, then TR and descend.

39 SO at XR, passing quarry on RHS. Descend with care.

40 TR at TJ, around sharp bend. Continue and pass through poled gate.

41 TL at TJ, to join road (60.5km/37.5 miles). Continue and pass Pluscarden Abbey on LHS, then Torrieston walks and picnic area on LHS.

42 SO through Miltonduff.

43 SO as road goes off to right (SP Dallas). Cross bridge over River Lossie.

44 TR at roundabout.

45 TR at TJ, onto main road. Then TR into station car park to complete the route.
73km (45.5 miles)

Route information

 Distance 74km (46 miles)

 Grade Moderate

 Terrain Well-surfaced, quiet roads and forestry tracks, suitable for fit cyclists who can cover the distance, on any type of bicycle. There are some gradual climbs. After prolonged rain the track across Monadh Mor can become boggy.

Time to allow 5–6 hours.

 Getting there by car Muir of Ord is on the A832, 9.5km (6 miles) west of the Tore roundabout on the A9. There is parking beside the railway station.

 Getting there by train Muir of Ord is on the Inverness/Thurso/Wick/Kyle of Lochalsh line run by Scotrail. There is a frequent service (although no Sunday service at the time of writing) and bicycles are carried for free – booking is essential. Telephone (0345) 484950 for information.

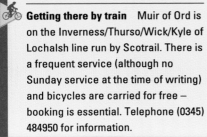

From Muir of Ord, following a designated cycle route to North Kessock, skirting the northern shores of the Beauly Firth. The route then climbs past the Black Isle Wildlife Centre for a fast descent to Munlochy. On eastwards, through the Black Isle towns of Avoch, Fortrose and Rosemarkie, with great views of the Moray Firth, to climb through Fairy Glen (legendary home of a black witch) and over the Milbuie

Ridge. A Forestry Commission track takes you through Mount Eagle for an exhilarating descent to Culbokie. The route then follows tracks across Monadh Mor, a Site of Special Scientific Interest, rich in ponds, bogs and associated wildlife. Minor roads take you back to Muir of Ord. Allow extra time to visit the attractions.

Places of interest along the route

Ⓐ North Kessock
North Kessock sits facing the narrows between the Beauly Firth and the Moray Firth. There are two wildlife exhibitions: **Dolphin and Seals of the Moray Firth**; and the **Red Kite Viewing Centre**. See route 3 for details.

Ⓑ Avoch Heritage Exhibition, Avoch
Describes the heritage and history of Avoch and the surrounding area. A village model with commentary creates the atmosphere of 1900. Open July to September, Monday–Saturday 1100–1700. Charge. Telephone (01381) 621125.

Ⓒ Glen Ord Distillery, Muir of Ord
The distillery has been licensed since 1838 and is the last surviving distillery in an area that once had nine. Tours of the distillery and exhibition on distilling and the Black Isle. Open all year, Monday–Friday 0930–1700; also July and August, Saturday 0930–1700, Sunday 1230–1700. Charge. Telephone (01463) 872004.

The route also passes the Black Isle Wildlife Centre, Fortrose Cathedral and the Groam House Museum in Rosemarkie – see route 3 and 10 for details.

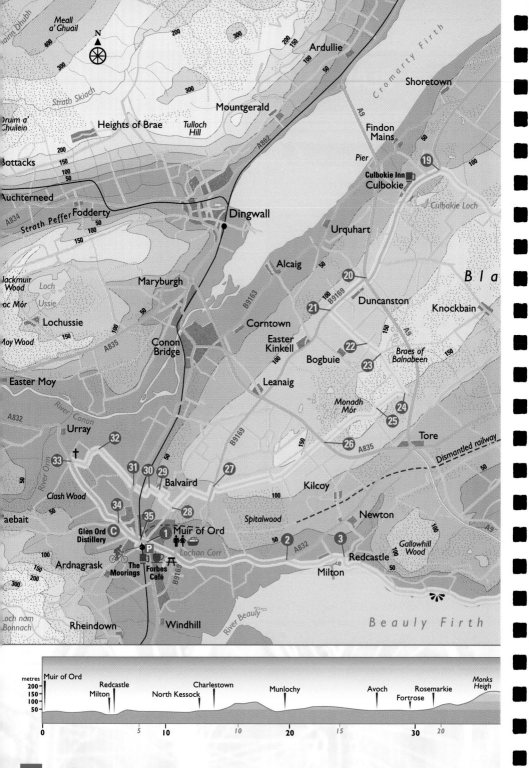

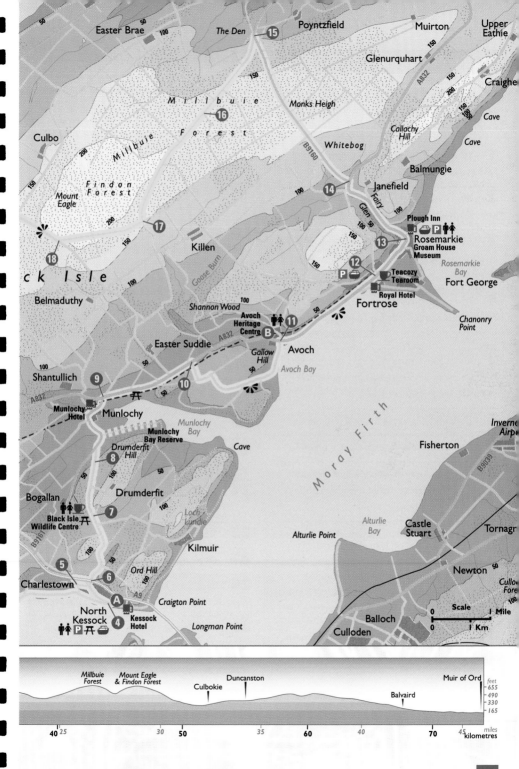

Route description

TR out of Muir of Ord railway station and immediately TR at TJ, SP Moray Firth Tourist Route. Cross railway bridge.

1 SO as road veers round to right, SP Fortrose/Cromarty A832.

2 TR, SP Redcastle/Charleston and North Kessock/Inverness cycle SP. *4.5km (3 miles)*

3 TR at TJ, no SP, descend to Beauly Firth coastal road. Continue along coast towards North Kessock.

4 To visit North Kessock, TR at TJ for 200m. To continue route, TL at TJ, Tore cycle SP.
12km (7.5 miles)

5 About 30m before A9 dual carriageway, TL, Tore cycle SP. TR and go through under-pass. TR, Munlochy cycle SP.

6 TL, Munlochy cycle SP, and join road.

7 Pass Black Isle Wildlife Centre on LHS.

8 Veer left down to junction and TR onto main road (B9161) for descent (16.5km/10.5 miles). Continue through Munlochy.

9 TR at TJ, SP Avoch/Fortrose/Rosemarkie/Cromarty A832.

10 TR, SP Corrachie/Avoch cycle SP. Continue towards Avoch. *21.5km (13.5 miles)*

11 TR, no SP (Avoch Heritage Centre is on LHS of this junction). Continue through Avoch and on to Fortrose. *25.5km (16 miles)*

12 Arrive Fortrose. Continue through town on A832 (cathedral is signposted) and on to Rosemarkie.

13 Arrive Rosemarkie (30km/18.5 miles). Pass Groam House Museum on RHS. Continue out of Rosemarkie on A832, staying on road up Fairy Glen.

14 TL, SP B9160 Jemimaville/Balblair. On descent, pass group of houses and telephone on RHS.

15 TL up road under pylons and climb.
37.5 km (23.5 miles)

16 Keep left on tarmac (as track goes right) until tarmac joins track. Continue SO this main track – do not turn off it.

17 TR at major track XR, onto main track (field on LHS and small unused track also to right). *44km (27.5 miles)*

18 TR onto unclassified tarmac road. Descend.

19 TL at TJ, SP Muir of Ord B9169 (50km/31 miles). Pass play park and common on LHS, then Culbokie Wood on LHS.

20 TR onto A9 and immediately TL, SP Easter Kinkell B9169.

21 TL, SP Braes of Balnabeen.
55km (34 miles)

22 SO and join track.

23 TR on track into forest.

24 Veer right and right again and cross Monadh Mor. *58.5km (36.5 miles)*

25 Keep left at junction, on Monadh Mor.

26 TR at TJ, and immediately TL, SP Wellhouse/Drynie Park.

27 TL at TJ, no SP (65km/40.5 miles). TR, SP Muir of Ord.

28	TR, SP Balvaird.
29	TL, no SP. *67.5km (42 miles)*
30	TL, no SP.
31	SO at XR with A9, SP Highfield.
32	Keep left as road swings round. *70km (43.5 miles)*
33	TL, no SP, but church on corner of junction. Continue towards Muir of Ord.
34	Pass Glen Ord Distillery on RHS.
35	TR, SP Station/Ardnagrash. Then TL into station to complete the route. *74km (46 miles)*

Food and drink

Refreshments are available in North Kessock, Fortrose and Rosemarkie and at the Black Isle Wildlife Centre.

Forbes Café, Muir of Ord
Open daily, 0830–2030.

The Moorings, Muir of Ord
Hotel serving bar meals and evening meals daily.

Munlochy Hotel, Munlochy
Tea, coffee and lunchtime bar meals.

Culbokie Inn, Culbokie
Bar meals available daily.

Cromarty Firth

Route 22
INVERNESS, FOYERS AND LOCH RUTHVEN

Route information

 Distance 78.5km (49 miles)

Grade Strenuous

Terrain Well-surfaced roads, suitable for any type of bicycle with low gears. Once out of Inverness, the roads are generally quiet but involve some stiff climbs. The route is suitable for all cyclists who can cope with the distance and the climbs.

Time to allow 6–7 hours.

Getting there by car Inverness is reached from the A9, A96 and A82. There is plenty of parking in the town and beside the railway station.

Getting there by train Inverness is at the hub of rail services from Aberdeen, Wick and Thurso, Kyle of Lochalsh and the south. Telephone (0345) 484950 for timetable information.

From Inverness to Dores and then along the eastern shore of Loch Ness to Foyers, with spectacular views over the loch to Drumnadrochit and imposing Urquhart Castle. From Foyers a steep climb passes the Falls of Foyers. A further climb follows the River Farigaig to Loch Ruthven. The route then passes through undulating, high moorland before a long and gradual descent to the banks of the River Ness and into Inverness. Allow extra time to visit the attractions along the way and to admire the spectacular scenery.

Places of interest along the route

A Inverness
Inverness is the main administrative centre of the Highlands and has plenty to offer the visitor. **Holm Mill** was established in 1798. Visitors can see the production of tartan and trace their clan and its history. Restaurant. Open all year, Monday–Saturday 0900–1730, Sunday 1000–1700. Admission free. Telephone (01463) 223311. See also routes 12 and 14.

B Falls of Foyers
Foyers is best known for its spectacular waterfalls. They are in two sections: the first falling 9m (29.5 feet); the second falling a spectacular 27m (88.5 feet). In 1894 the water power was harnessed in a pioneering hydro-electric plant to power a nearby aluminium factory.

C Loch Ruthven
A RSPB nature reserve. Black grouse are often seen in the surrounding moors, and a hide gives you the chance to observe ospreys, peregrines, hen harriers and rare Slovonian grebes in their natural habitats. Open all year at all reasonable times. Admission free. Telephone (01463) 715000.

D Brin School Fields Herb Nursery, Brin
Specialising in herbs and wild flowers, all grown at 213m (700 feet) above sea level. Display gardens and organised events. Also bulbs, cottage garden plants, salads and herbs. Open mid March to October, Monday–Saturday 0900–1800, Sunday 1400–1700. Admission free.

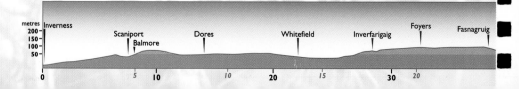

Route description

From the main entrance of Inverness railway station, SO across the main road and down Union Street (a one way street). TL at TJ into Church Street. Walk across the 20m of pedestrian precinct.

1 TR into Bridge Street (opposite the Tourist Information Centre – Inverness Museum/Art Gallery and castle are behind the TIC). TL at traffic lights, along road parallel to the River Ness.

2 TR and continue on road alongside river out of Inverness, passing Holm Mill on RHS. Continue on B862 to Dores.

3 In Dores, TR, SP Foyers (13.5km/8.5 miles) and continue on B852, alongside Loch Ness towards Foyers.

4 SO past forestry houses (27km/17 miles). Pass SP for Inverfarigaig picnic site/toilets/walks/information.

5 SO through Foyers and climb (31.5 km/19.5 miles). Pass Falls of Foyers on RHS.

6 TL, SP Glenlia B862.

7 SO, no SP.

8 TL, SP Inverfarigaig (35.5km/22 miles). Pass toilets (LHS) and river walks (RHS).

9 TR, no SP. Then TR again, no SP, and continue. **38km (23.5 miles)**

10 TL, no SP. **45.5km (28.5 miles)**

11 TR, SP RSPB Loch Ruthven Nature Reserve. **49km (30.5 miles)**

12 Pass head of Loch Ruthven on RHS. **55km (34 miles)**

13 TL at TJ onto B851, no SP. Continue on this road, passing the herb nursery on LHS.

14 TL, SP Dunlichity.

15 Veer left, no SP. **60km (37.5 miles)**

16 SO, no SP.

17 TR, SP Bunachton (opposite this junction is Dunlichity Church, where Jacobite soldiers are thought to have sharpened their swords on the gravestones before the Battle of Culloden – some of the gravestones have score marks on them).

18 TL, SP Bunachton (63.5km/39.5 miles), and continue on this road.

19 TR at TJ, no SP. **71km (44 miles)**

20 SO, SP Inverness.

21 SO at roundabout, SP Town Centre.

22 TR at TJ, SP Town Centre (76km/47 miles). Follow riverside road back into Inverness.

23 TR at traffic lights into Bridge Street. As road turns to right by TIC, continue SO and walk through pedestrianised area of High Street.

24 TL again, through pedestrianised area of Inglis Street. TL to join Academy Street. TR, SP Station, to complete the route.
78.5km (49 miles)

Food and drink

There is plenty of choice in Inverness and Foyers has a tearoom, hotel and shop (open seasonally).

Schoolroom Tearoom, Brin
Winner of a healthy eating award, the tearoom offers salads, homemade soups, homebaking and other refreshments. Open as per Brin School Fields Herb Nursery.

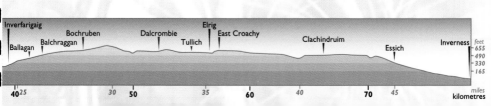

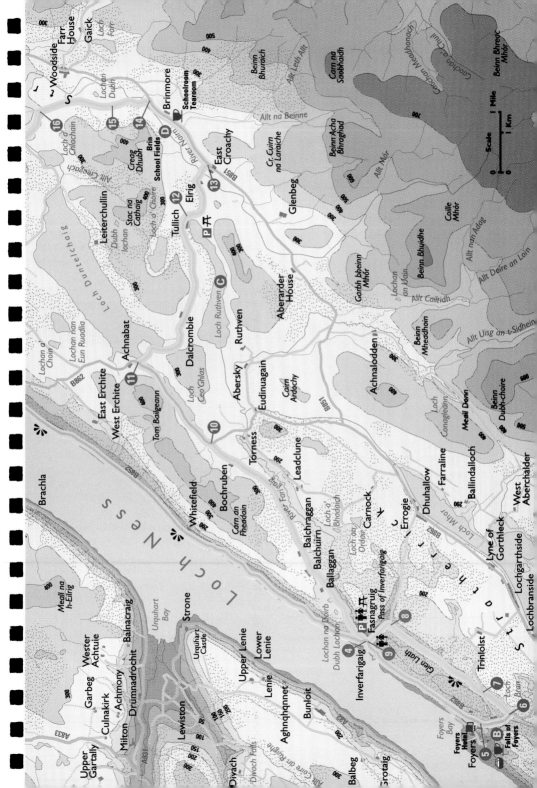

TOMINTOUL, BALLINDALLOCH AND THE SPEYSIDE WAY

Route information

Distance 80.5km (50 miles)

Grade Moderate

Terrain Well-surfaced roads and a disused railway line (part of the Speyside Way), suitable for any type of bicycle with low gears to cope with the climbs. The section of route along the Speyside Way between Ballindalloch and Aberlour is suitable for all cyclists, but the total distance and hilly nature of the rest of the route make it suitable for more experienced cyclists who can cope with the distance and hills.

Time to allow 6–7 hours.

Getting there by car Tomintoul is on the A939 Grantown-on-Spey to Braemar road. There is parking in the village square, in a car park just off the main street, and at the Glenlivet Estate Office/Information Centre at the top (southern) end of the village.

Getting there by train There is no practical rail access to this route. Aviemore and Carrbridge are the nearest railway stations, both approximately 32km (20 miles) away.

From Tomintoul the route descends through the Glenlivet Estate, following the Conglass Water to its convergence with the River Avon. On, following the River Avon to its meeting with the

mighty River Spey at Ballindalloch. Between Ballindalloch and Aberlour, the route joins the Speyside Way. The old railway line is relatively flat and offers spectacular views. From Aberlour the route starts the return climb to Tomintoul, passing over Glack Harnes (the saddle between Ben Rinnes and Meikle Conval – the two striking hills in this area). Turning westwards the route continues to climb back to Tomintoul. For further information the Speyside Way, see page 8.

Places of interest along the route

A Tomintoul

Tomintoul lies between the Ladder and Cromdale Hills, at the edge of the Cairngorms. See route 13 for information.

B Ballindalloch

Ballindalloch Castle family home of the Macpherson-Grants since 1546, is bordered by the Rivers Avon and Spey. The spectacular grounds contain rock and rose gardens, a doocot and extensive lawns. Tearoom. Open Good Friday to end September 1000–1700. Charge. Telephone (01340) 500206. **Cragganmore Distillery** visitor centre contains a fascinating collection of artefacts dating back to the days of John Smith who founded Cragganmore in 1869. Distillery tours. Open June to September, Monday–Thursday. Charge. Telephone for times of tours on (01807) 500202.

C The Village Store, Aberlour

Bought by Mr Affie Macintyre in 1922, and run as a general store until 1978, this is a perfectly preserved village store of yesteryear. Open mid-February to mid-January, Monday–Friday 1000–

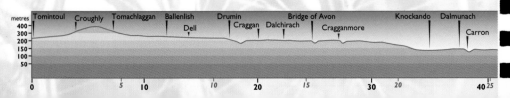

1700, Sunday 1330–1700. Admission by donation. Telephone (01340) 871243.

The route also passes the Museum of Scottish Country Life in Drumin. See route 14 for details.

Route description

Start from Glenlivet Estate Office/Information Centre. TR out of car park and descend towards village centre.

1 TR, SP Braemar A939/Dufftown B9008.

2 TL, SP Croughly.

3 TR onto B9136, no SP. **7km (4.5 miles)**

4 SO, SP Glenlivet 4 B9136 (11km/7 miles). Continue, passing picnic sites on RHS and Museum of Country Life on LHS.

5 TL (200m after museum), no SP. Descend steeply to cross river and then climb (16.5km/ 10.5 miles). TL at TJ, no SP, onto B9008 and continue on this road.

6 To visit Ballindalloch Castle, TR at TJ (at hairpin bend), SP Elgin. Continue and TL, SP Ballindalloch Castle and Grounds (24km/15 miles). After visit, retrace to entrance, TL, continue and SO at junction, SP Grantown-on-Spey.

Otherwise, TL at TJ, SP Grantown-on-Spey.

7 TR with care, SP Speyside Way/ Cragganmore B9137. Pass Cragganmore Distillery on LHS.

8 Pass through Speyside Way car park and TR to join Speyside Way (29.5km/18.5 miles). Follow SP Speyside Way to Aberlour.

9 Arrive car park in Aberlour and continue SO, following car park access road into Aberlour (45.5km/28.5 miles). Pass toilets and small café in old station on LHS.

10 TR up to Aberlour main street (the Village Store is on LHS of village square) and TR at XR at main street. Leave village, crossing river.

11 TL, no SP (first TL after crossing river – a sharp hairpin-like turn). Start to climb out of Aberlour.

12 SO past junction on right, then SO past junction on left.

13 SO, no SP.

14 LHF at junction, staying on road (51km/31.5 miles). Climb over Glack Harnes (Ben Rinnes on RHS).

15 TR at TJ, no SP, and continue along Glen Rinnes on B9009. **55km (34 miles)**

16 TL at TJ, SP Tomintoul B9008 (66.5km/41.5 miles). Continue on this road.

17 SO, SP Tomintoul A939.
79.5km (49.5 miles)

18 TL at TJ in Tomintoul, and climb through village. TL to finish route at Glenlivet Estate Office/Information Centre. **80.5km (50 miles)**

Food and drink

There is a coffee shop at Glenlivet Distillery and a shop in Tomnavoulin.

Clockhouse Restaurant, Tomintoul
In the village square, serving breakfasts, snacks and meals.

Glen Avon Hotel, Tomintoul
Cozy open fire. Bar meals served daily 1200–1430 and 1730–2000. Cyclists welcome.

Old Pantry, Aberlour
Delicious homebakes, snacks and meals.

Croft Inn, Glenlivet
Peaceful country pub nestling under Ben Rinnes. Open fire in winter, garden seating in summer. Extensive bar menu and vast range of local malt whiskies.

Milltown of Edinvillie Sheandow Lynemore Aultbeg Rinaitin Tervieside Auchbreck Tomnavoulin Knockandhu Tomintoul

Aberlour

feet
1310
980
655
490
330
165

30 50   35   60   40   70   45   80 50 miles
kilometres

NAIRN, DULSIE BRIDGE AND LOCHINDORB

Route information

Distance   102km (63.5 miles)

Grade   Moderate

Terrain   Well-surfaced roads (and a short section of good track), suitable for all cyclists (including older children with good road skills) who can cope with the distance and prolonged climb, on any type of bicycle. Although the route involves some sections of A road, these are generally quiet. The area between Cawdor and Logie Steading is remote, with no refreshment facilities, and cyclists should carry food and drink.

Time to allow   7–8 hours.

Getting there by car   Nairn is on the A96 Inverness to Aberdeen road. There is parking in the town, beside the railway station.

Getting there by train   Nairn is on the Aberdeen to Inverness line run by Scotrail. There is a frequent service and bicycles are carried free of charge – booking is essential. Telephone (0345) 484950 for information.

From Nairn to Cawdor, following the River Nairn through rolling farmland and woodland. At Cawdor the route joins the old Fort George to Braemar military road and starts to climb, initially through farmland and woodland and then over remote moorland towards Drynachan. After a long climb, you are rewarded with a spectacular winding descent to the River Findhorn. Turning eastwards, the route takes an undulating, wooded road alongside the river, eventually crossing spectacular Dulsie Bridge, where ospreys and red kites can often be seen (cyclists should stop north of the bridge and walk back to view the river). The road continues to climb over Dava Moor, and circles Lochindorb, a remote loch with 14th-century castle, before starting a long descent, passing the spectacular beauty spots of Randolph's Leap and Sluie Walks, eventually reaching Forres. From Forres the route follows sections of the Aberdeen to Inverness bike route 1, crossing the River Findhorn and passing through the historic village of Auldearn before returning to Nairn. Allow extra time for visiting the numerous attractions along the way.

Route description

Starting from Nairn station, TR out of the car park for 100m. TR at TJ into Cawdor Road and cycle under railway bridge.

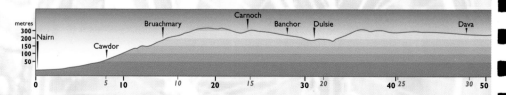

1 SO, SP Cawdor B9090, and continue on this road.

2 TR at TJ, SP Cawdor B9090, and continue. *4km (2.5 miles)*

3 TL, SP Cawdor Castle and pass castle entrance on RHS.

4 SO at XR, SP Dulsie Bridge $7^3/4$. *9.5km (6 miles)*

5 SO at XR, SP Dulsie Bridge $6^1/2$.

6 TR, SP Drynachan $4^1/2$ (15.5km/9.5 miles) for steep, winding descent to River Findhorn.

7 TL and follow river downstream. *23km (14.5 miles)*

8 TR at TJ, SP Dulsie Bridge $1/4$ (31km/ 19 miles). Cross Dulsie Bridge and continue.

9 TR at XR onto B9007, SP Carrbridge (old SP 50m before junction). *34km (21 miles)*

10 TL, SP Lochindorb. Pass Lochindorb and continue on this road.

11 TL at TJ, no SP. *48.5km (30 miles)*

12 LHF, SP Nairn A939, and continue.

13 TR WITH CARE at XR, SP Forres 11 B9007. *58km (36 miles)*

14 Opposite Relugas House (private) on LHS are paths to Randolph's Leap.

15 TL to visit Logie Steading. Otherwise, continue SO. *65.5km (40.5 miles)*

16 TL at TJ, SP Forres 6 A940. Pass Sluie Walks. Continue.

17 TR, SP Dallas Dhu Distillery. *72.5km (45 miles)*

18 To visit Dallas Dhu Distillery, TR at TJ for 100m. Otherwise, TL at TJ to continue route.

19 TR at TJ in Forres. *75.5km (47 miles)*

20 Take third exit at roundabout (between garage and river) and immediately TR alongside river. SO as road veers right over bridge.

21 Take track up to road and use crossing across busy A96. TR and rejoin road to cross level crossing.

22 TL up Waterford Road (before distillery).

23 TL by transmitter, SP bike 1, onto track into forest. TL at TJ by river, and head up river.

24 Keep right as small tracks go off to left.

25 TR at TJ and follow main track.

26 TR and cross bailey bridge. Cycle down track into village, where TL and join tarmac.

27 TR at TJ, SP bike 1.

28 LHF, SP bike 1/Culbin/Dyke/Kintessack. *81km (50.5 miles)*

29 LHF, SP bike 1/Dyke/Kintessack. Continue through Kintessack.

30 SO, SP bike 1/Dyke.

31 TR at TJ, SP bike 1/Dyke/Brodie.

32 To visit Brodie Castle (an extra 0.5km/ 0.3 mile), TR, SP Brodie Castle. After visit, leave along one way system and TR to rejoin route at direction 33.

To visit Small World (an extra 2km/1 mile), TL then TR at TJ and immediately TL. Continue to visitor centre. Retrace route to XR opposite Brodie Castle entrance and TL to continue route.

Otherwise, SO to continue route.

33 TR at TJ, SP bike 1. Pass woodland walks, bird hide and picnic area on LHS.

34 TL at TJ, SP bike 1/Nairn.

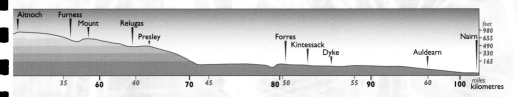

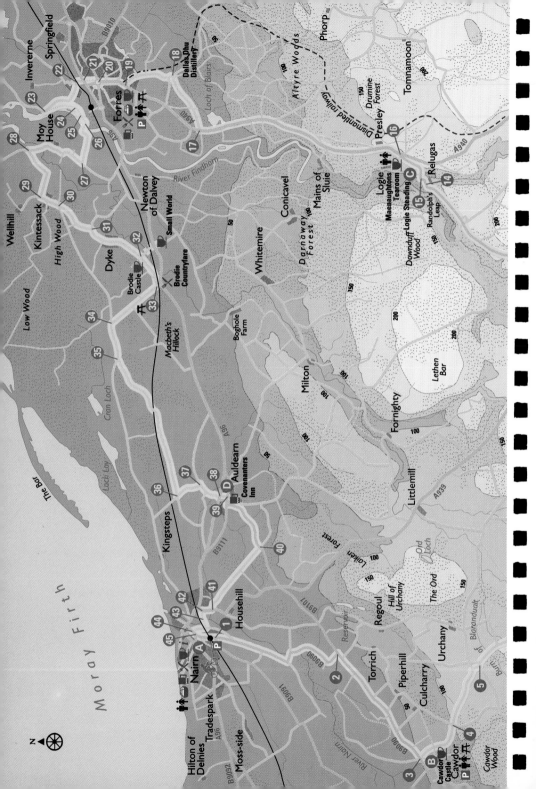

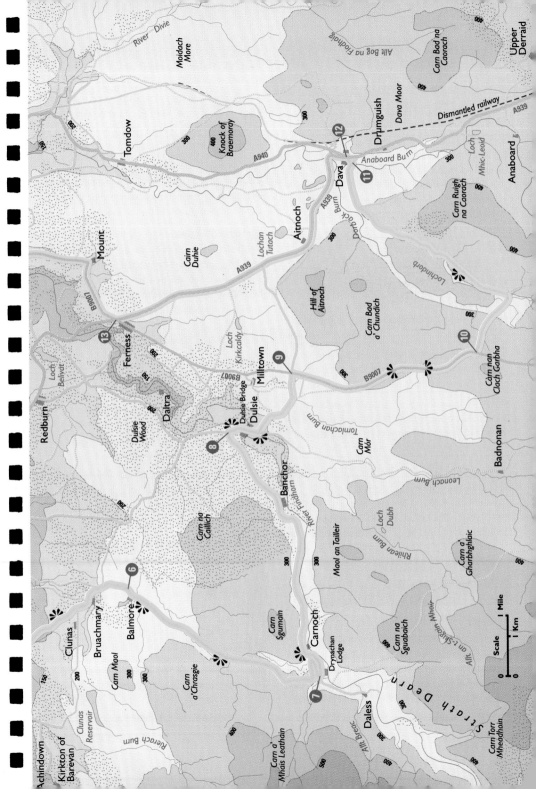

35 TL as road swings to right, no SP (but old SP Nairn pointing right).

36 TL at XR, SP Auldearn 1.

37 TR at TJ, no SP.

38 Arrive TJ with busy A96. TR WITH CARE and immediately TL up path which loops around to top of steps beside church in Auldearn (96km/59.5 miles) SO by church and descend into Auldearn. (To visit Boath Doocot, TR beside church and climb through houses. TR at top, past green to doocot entrance in corner. Retrace to church).

39 TR at TJ, opposite bollards. TL beside Covenanters Inn, SP Cawdor Castle.

40 TR at XR SP (down by trees). Cycle through industrial estate.

41 TR at TJ and climb towards graveyard.
100.5km (62.5 miles)

42 TL into park (just before graveyard), SP bike 1/Town Centre/Station. Follow path around edge of graveyard and past small bridge on left.

43 TL over bridge, SP bike1/Town Centre/ Station. Continue SO and follow path past pavilion and up between houses. TR at TJ between houses, no SP, and cycle under railway bridge.

44 TL at TJ in Nairn High Street.

45 TL (as main road swings to right), SP Cawdor/Croy B9009. Pass war memorial on LHS and then TR SP Station. TL into the station to complete the route. *102km (63.5 miles)*

Places of interest along the route

A Nairn
A traditional fishing town, Nairn is today well-known as a holiday resort. There are beautiful sandy beaches, extensive leisure facilities, two local museums, and access to Culbin Forest/ Sands (see route 6 for details). **Nairn Fishertown Museum** includes a reconstructed fisherman's house and gives visitors an insight into the heritage of the local fishing community. The 130-year-old **Nairn Museum** includes displays on natural history, minerals, fossils, and local people, such as Augustus Grant who discovered the source of the Nile. For further information, telephone Nairn Tourist Information Centre on (01667) 452753.

B Cawdor Castle, Cawdor
Cawdor Castle, linked to Shakespeare's *Macbeth*, is one of the most romantic castles in Scotland. See route 18 for details.

C Logie Steading
Originally built in 1920 as a model farm, the steading has been converted into craft workshops. Also walled garden and an art gallery. MacNaughtons Tearoom offers meals made from local produce. Some workshops open all year, others seasonally, Tuesday–Sunday 1030–1700. Admission free. Telephone (01309) 611378.

D Auldearn
Auldearn was the site where the Earl of Montrose raised the Royal Standard (on behalf of Charles I) and defeated the Covenanters in 1645. The 17th-century Boath Doocot in Auldearn overlooks the battlefield and has an explanatory board. Open all year, daily. Charge.

The route also passes Small World and for information in this and on Forres and Brodie, see route 6.

Food and drink

Plenty of choice in Nairn and Forres, and tearooms at Cawdor and Brodie castles.

X Brodie Countryfare, Brodie
Restaurant featuring local Scottish ingredients on an extensive menu.

Covenanters Inn, Auldearn
Adjacent to the historic battlefield, offering snacks and meals.

Route 25
LOCH NESS CIRCUIT – A GRANDE RANDONNÉE

Route information

 Distance 128km (79.5 miles)

Grade Strenuous

Terrain Well-surfaced roads, forestry tracks and a purpose built cycle track (which can be rough), only suitable for experienced cyclists on mountain bikes or sturdy touring bikes with low gears and good brakes – most of the roads and tracks are quiet but involve steep climbs and descents. A purpose built link is planned to run between Drumnadrochit and Abriachan and this will be an alternative to the route through Glen Convinth.

 Time to allow 8–10 hours.

 Getting there by car Inverness is reached from the A9, A96 and A82. There is plenty of parking in the town and beside the railway station.

Getting there by train Inverness is at the hub of rail services from Aberdeen, Wick and Thurso, Kyle of Lochalsh and the south. Telephone (0345) 484950 for further information.

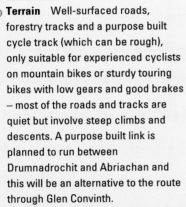

A spectacular route around Loch Ness, using the Great Glen Cycle Route down the western side of the loch and quiet minor roads along the eastern shore. The route follows the River Ness out of Inverness and crosses the Caledonian Canal. A steep climb up to the Aird Hills through Blackfold and Abriachan is rewarded with grand views over the northern Highlands, before an undulating route through Glen Convinth to Drumnadrochit. The route then follows forestry tracks (many purpose built) down the western side of the loch, via Invermoriston to Fort Augustus. The tracks climb high above the loch and give excellent views. At Fort Augustus the route crosses the Caledonian Canal a second time and climbs up one of General Wade's military roads. The views are again spectacular. A breathtaking descent takes you to Foyers and the eastern shores of Loch Ness. Then along the shore to Dores and on through undulating countryside and woodland, before returning to Inverness. Allow extra time to visit the attractions. This route could be completed over two days, staying overnight at Loch Ness Youth Hostel, or in Fort Augustus – telephone the Tourist Information Centre in Fort Augustus for further information on (01320) 366367.

The Great Glen Cycle Route (GGCR) was initiated by the Forestry Commission to take cyclists away from the busy A82 onto forest roads, tracks and sections of the Caledonian Canal towpath. At present the route links Fort William to Drumnadrochit, with development of the northern section (from Drumnadrochit to Inverness) continuing. There are waymark posts (green mountain bikes) along the route, information boards at the start of each section of track and signposts at junctions with public roads. Sections of the route have been purpose-built and the surfaces can be rough and steep. The Forestry Commission publishes a leaflet giving general guidance and describing the route stage-by-stage. See page 8 for further information.

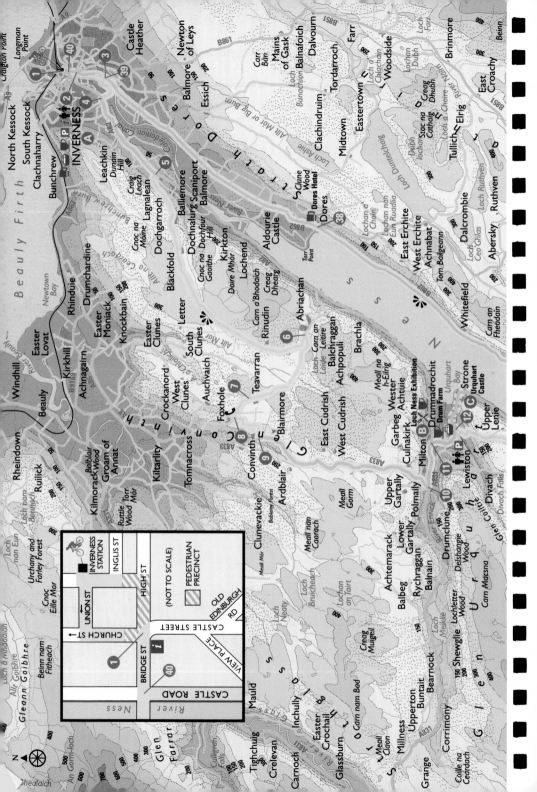

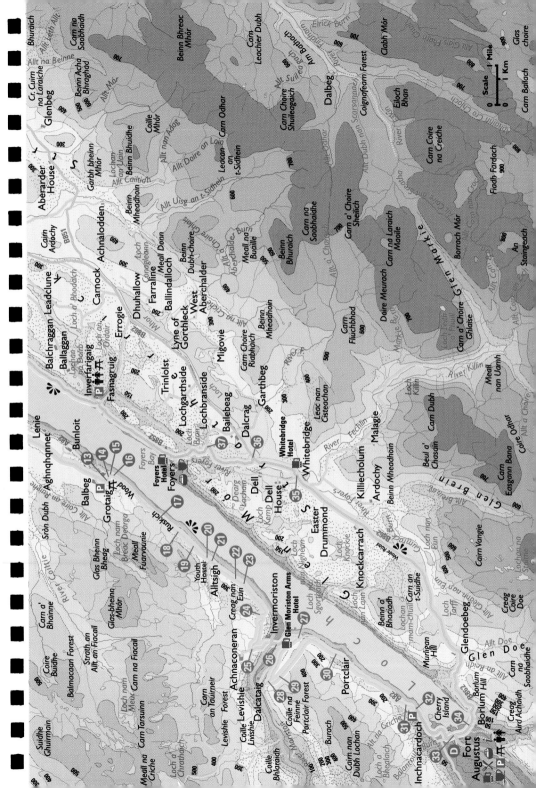

Places of interest along the route

A Inverness
Inverness has long been the site of a settlement – remains dating from the Bronze Age have been discovered in the city. Today, Inverness is the main adminsitrative centre of the Highlands. See routes 12 and 14 for information.

B Drumnadrochit
Drumnadrochit sits by the side of the largest bay on Loch Ness. See route 12 for information.

C Urquhart Castle, Strone Point
The ruined remains of one of Scotland's largest castles. Also see route 12.

D Fort Augustus
Fort Augustus sits at the entrance to the Caledonian Canal, at the south west end of Loch Ness: a lighthouse marks the canal entrance. The village grew up around the fort, built in 1730 by General Wade and later incorporated into the 19th-century Benedictine monastery. The **Clansman Centre** illustrates the life of a Highland family in the 17th century. Craft shop, restaurant and picnic area. Open all year, daily 0900–1700 (reduced hours in winter). Charge. Telephone (01320) 366233.

Route description

From the main entrance of Inverness railway station, SO across main road and down Union Street (a one way street). TL at TJ into Church Street and walk across the 20m of pedestrian precinct.

1 TR into Bridge Street (opposite Tourist Information Centre – Inverness Museum/Art Gallery and castle are behind TIC). TL at traffic lights and follow River Ness. The Kiltmaker Visitor Centre is across the bridge in the far right corner.

2 TR and follow road next to the river.

3 TR and walk across footbridge, SP No Cycling. TL after bridge and continue parallel to river, passing Bught Park.

4 TL at TJ, SP GGCR/Drumnadrochit. Cross canal and continue, WITH CARE, along busy A82. (Just after the canal bridge, on LHS, is access point for Jacobite Cruises.)

5 TR, WITH CARE, SP Abriachan/Blackfold, and continue on this road. *6.5km (4 miles)*

6 TR, SP Foxhole/Beauly, and continue past Loch Laide. *17.5km (11 miles)*

7 TL at TJ, no SP (SP back the way for Drum- nadrochit via Loch Ness). *21.5km (13.5 miles)*

8 TL (on descent, 30m before old school and telephone box on RHS), no SP. Descend.

9 TL at TJ (after descent) onto A833. Continue through Glen Convinth.
24.5km (15 miles)

10 TL at TJ, SP Drumnadrochit A831.
32km (20 miles)

11 TR at TJ in Drumnadrochit, SP Fort William A82 (35.5km/22 miles). On LHS of junction is Loch Ness Monster Exhibition Centre; Drum Farm is 200m after junction on LHS.

12 To visit Urquhart Castle (adds 4km/ 2.5 miles to total distance along busy section of A82) continue SO WITH CARE. Retrace to junction and TL, SP Clunebeg.

Otherwise, to continue route, TR ,WITH CARE, SP Clunebeg (no GGCR SP). Continue up steep hill to end of road.

13 TL between car park and picnic site, SP GGCR. Continue through gate and down track.
43km (27 miles)

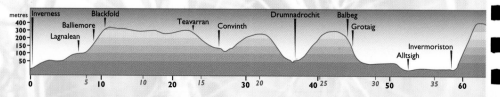

14 Through gate and TR (track comes in from left). Cross burn via bridge. Continue through clearing and next gate. Descend through trees and gate, SP GGCR.

15 Join large track and TR, SP GGCR.

16 RHF at turning area and up track, SP GGCR. **45km (28 miles)**

17 TL to join main forest track (excellent views but care as there are some tricky narrow sections).

18 TL, SP GGCR, for very steep descent.

19 TR, SP GGCR (50.5km/31.5 miles). Stay on main track and descend.

20 To access Loch Ness Youth Hostel, TL, SP Youth Hostel. To continue route, SO, SP GGCR.

21 SO, SP GGCR.

22 Veer right up hill, SP GGCR.

23 Pass stone cave shelter on RHS, and follow SP GGCR. **55.5km (34.5 miles)**

24 TR off main track onto smaller track going up hill, SP GGCR. Climb steeply and TL onto main track, SP GGCR. TL, SP GGCR.

25 TL onto tarmac, SP GGCR.

26 TL onto main road, SP Fort Augustus. Cycle into Invermoriston and TR, no SP.

27 TR, SP GGCR/Dalcataig. Continue to end of road and through gate. **59.5km (37 miles)**

28 TL, SP GGCR, and through gate.

29 LHF, SP GGCR.

30 RHF, SP GGCR. **65km (40.5 miles)**

31 SO, SP GGCR (71km/44 miles). Continue on main track and descend to Allt Na Criche car park.

32 TR WITH CARE at TJ onto busy section of A82, SP GGCR. Continue through Fort Augustus, crossing canal. (The Clansman Centre is on LHS after canal.)

33 TL, SP Loch Ness Trail B862.

34 Continue SO on B862 (75.5km/47 miles), for long, steep climb (on one of General Wade's military roads).

35 Pass through Whitebridge. **89km (55.5 miles)**

36 TL just beside graveyard, SP Foyers B852.

37 TL, no SP (94km/58.5 miles). Continue through Foyers (passing Falls of Foyer on LHS) and Inverfarigaig (where there are forest walks and picnic areas – SP TR). **100km (62 miles)**

38 Arrive Dores. TL at TJ, SP Inverness. Continue into Inverness. **114km (71 miles)**

39 Into Inverness, keeping to road that runs parallel to river (Island Bank Road, Ladies Walk, Ness Walk, Ness Bank and Castle Road). **125.5km (78 miles)**

40 TR at traffic lights, into Bridge Street. Pass Tourist Information Centre and walk SO up the pedestrianised High Street. TL into Inglis Street and TL into Academy Street. TR, SP Station, to finish the route. **128km (79.5 miles)**

Food and drink

Plenty of choice in Inverness and Fort Augustus, and a tearoom and hotel in Foyers. Refreshments are also available at Drumnadrochit Hotel, Drum Farm and the Clansman Centre.

Glen Moriston Arms Hotel, Invermoriston
Bar meals available in this traditional hotel.

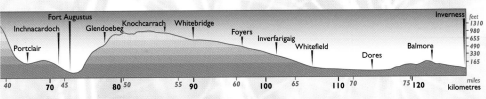

THE CTC

The CTC is Britain's largest national cycling organisation. Founded in 1878, the CTC has over 65,000 members and affiliates throughout the UK, and around 230 local groups. The CTC provides essential services for all leisure cyclists, whether riding on- or off-road, and works to promote cycling and protect cyclists' interests.

Free technical and touring advice

CTC membership makes day-to-day cycling easier. A resident expert cycling engineer answers technical queries about cycle buying, maintenance and equipment. And if you get ambitious about your cycling, the CTC's Touring Department has reams of information about cycling anywhere from Avon to Zimbabwe. Then, when it comes to getting kitted out, the CTC's mail order shop sells a wide variety of clothing and accessories in addition to books, maps and guidebooks, including other titles from HarperCollins Publishers.

CTC Helpdesk – telephone (01483) 417217

CTC members also receive *Cycle Touring and Campaigning* magazine free six times a year. *CT&C* takes pride in its journalistic independence. With reports on cycle trips all over the globe, forensic tests on bikes and equipment, and the most vigorous and effective pro-bike campaigning stance anywhere, *CT&C* is required reading for any cyclist.

CTC membership costs from £15 p.a.

It is not just members who benefit. The CTC works on behalf of all Britain's 22 million cycle owners. Its effective campaigning at national level helped to create the Government's National Cycling Strategy. It is lobbying for lower speed limits on country lanes; campaigning so that you can carry bikes on trains; working with Local Authorities to make towns more cycle-friendly, to ensure that roads are designed to meet cyclists' needs and kept well maintained; making sure that bridleways are kept open; and negotiating cyclists' access to canal towpaths.

Whatever kind of cyclist you are – mountain biker, Sunday potterer, bicycle commuter, or out for the day with your family – cycling is easier and safer with the CTC's knowledge and services in your saddlebag. The CTC is the essential accessory for every cyclist!

For further information contact:
CTC
69 Meadrow
Godalming
Surrey
GU7 3HS

Telephone (01483) 417217
Fax (01483) 426994
e-mail: cycling@ctc.org.uk
Website: http://www.ctc.org.uk